How to Achieve Financial Freedom

How to Achieve Financial Freedom

Create Enough Wealth to Stop Working

EOIN McGEE

First published in the UK in 2026 by Eriu
An imprint of Bonnier Books UK
5th Floor, HYLO, 105 Bunhill Row,
London, EC1Y 8LZ

Copyright © Eoin McGee, 2026

All rights reserved.

No part of this publication may be reproduced, stored or transmitted in any form or by any means, electronic, mechanical, photocopying or otherwise, without the prior written permission of the publisher.

The right of Eoin McGee to be identified as Author of this work has been asserted by him in accordance with the Copyright, Designs and Patents Act, 1988.

This book is a work of Non-Fiction. Some names may have been changed to respect the privacy of those mentioned.

A CIP catalogue record for this book is available from the British Library.

Trade Paperback ISBN: 978-1-80444-334-7

Also available as an ebook and an audiobook

1 3 5 7 9 10 8 6 4 2

Design and Typeset by Envy Design
Printed and bound by CPI (UK) Ltd, Croydon CR0 4YY

Every reasonable effort has been made to trace copyright holders of material reproduced in this book, but if any have been inadvertently overlooked the publishers would be glad to hear from them.

The authorised representative in the EEA is
Bonnier Books UK (Ireland) Limited.
Registered office address:
Block B, The Crescent Building
Northwood, Santry
Dublin 9, D09 C6X8, Ireland
compliance@bonnierbooks.ie

www.bonnierbooks.co.uk

Contents

Introduction	1
What life do you want to live?	4
Where do you start?	31
The big mistakes	32
30 big mistakes	41
1. Trying to do too much in one go	41
2. Taking on debt	49
3. Thinking a new car is a requirement	58
4. Not regularly checking your accounts/spending	65
5. Not having your money working as hard as you do	66
6. Deciding you are not good with money	67
7. Not educating yourself	69
8. Not being honest	70
9. Thinking the big moves are more impactful than the small ones	71

10. Having a little bit of knowledge	74
11. Getting advice from the wrong place	76
12. Not writing stuff down	79
13. Leaving the back door open	81
14. Paying too much tax	82
15. Making emotional decisions instead of financial ones	84
16. Allowing lifestyle creep to kick in	87
17. Wallet leakage	89
18. Picking the wrong partner	92
19. Not having a financial plan	99
20. Deciding when to get into bed together (financially)	100
21. Not saving	103
22. Not automating stuff	106
23. Comparing yourself to others	108
24. Surrounding yourself with the wrong people – personally and professionally	111
25. Buying things, not time	113
26. Not naming your savings	115
27. Thinking more money will fix bad habits	116
28. Thinking you will be happy when you have more money	119
29. Thinking the future is bright	123
30. Thinking the route to financial freedom is to work harder	126

Outside influences	129
Price anchoring	133
Scarcity	136
Reciprocity bias	140
Commitment bias	141
Endowment effect	143
Loss aversion	145
Primacy bias	148
Recency bias	150
Framing effect	153
Social proof trigger	155
Community trigger	160
Heuristics and biases summary	165
Establishing where you are	169
Your net worth	169
Your cashflow	176
Where are you going?	179
Your buffer	181
Short-term goals	184
Medium-term goals	185
Tackling debt	186
The secret savings plan	187
Putting your surplus income to work	190
Investing your money	193
Investing mistakes	193
Summary	212

Your master plan	213
The five-year rule	213
Parkinson's law	214
What ifs	215
How do I do all the maths?	216
Revisiting your plan	237
Keeping up to date	237
Consider using an adviser	238
Financial stress	241
Conclusion	245
Acknowledgements	247

Introduction

Beep … beep … beep …

I gradually become aware of the noise. I'm confused. I open my eyes, and I'm looking at a ceiling with those funny square Styrofoam-like tiles. I am sore. I don't really know where I am sore. I am very uncomfortable. I look around and I fall asleep again.

It is 4 May 2018 and I am in A&E in Portlaoise Hospital. At this stage I don't know why. The next 24 hours is a blur. Every time I open my eyes there's a different person – a doctor, a friend, a paramedic – with me. I hear someone talking about a helicopter and then I'm in an ambulance, being transferred to Beaumont.

I didn't know then, or at least I didn't comprehend, that I was on my way for brain surgery. My life was about to change for ever.

The night before I had been at my friend Tony's work leaving dinner in Carlow. I'd had a few drinks, but I was not drunk.

When I got out of the taxi at the hotel, I fell – I don't know why or how – and the first thing to hit the ground was my head. I cracked my skull in three places, and it set off a brain bleed that would require surgery.

The surgery happened on a Friday and I woke up on Saturday morning. For the first time in 36 hours I was somewhat coherent. The surgeon was at the end of my bed talking to his team, telling them where things were at with me. I didn't realise it, but at that time I was still being monitored because they expected I would need more surgery.

Without turning to me at all, the surgeon was about to leave the ward when I called him back. 'Sorry, doctor, can I ask when can I go back to work?'

He looked at me with what I now realise was frustration and said dismissively, 'I don't know – six to eight weeks?', and he turned to leave. I called after him, 'Sorry, sorry, doctor, you don't understand. I work for myself; I need to know when I will be able to go back to work.'

There was no doubting his frustration when he walked back to me a second time. He said, very directly, 'No, *you* don't understand. I have you here and you are alive.'

It was at this point that it dawned on me. I had nearly died. In fact, I was not out of the woods yet. But my biggest worry was when I could get back to work. Here I was in a hospital bed worrying about getting back to work and the surgeon who had saved my life was still worrying about getting me through.

For context, at that time, Prosperous (the financial planning firm I founded in 2008) had three staff. One had been with me for years but had gone on maternity leave a couple of weeks before; one had been with me a year or so; and the third had only joined the firm a week before.

I had a few hours to myself that morning before I saw or spoke to anyone. Sitting there, having escaped death, in pain and recovering from surgery, I had a fleeting but immensely striking thought, one that gave me clarity on so many things in my life. I thought about the people in my life I loved and the things I loved to do. The places I loved to be, the things I wanted to experience and the things I wanted to achieve. I also thought about the things I wanted to change in my life.

As I write this, I look back on what my life has been like since that accident and I ask myself, if I could, would I go back and change what happened? No, I wouldn't. Horrible and all as it was, I wouldn't change the fact that it happened. I realise that I'm incredibly fortunate not to have any ongoing symptoms or problems because of my fall. Maybe if I did I would think differently, but these were the cards I was dealt, and I would not change them.

I was under the care of a brilliant team and I guess some luck came into it too. I got all the benefit of my sudden mental clarity. I'd had a literal wake-up call from the surgeon standing at the end of my bed. The world aligned to give me those few hours alone, thinking about the fact that I'd almost had my life taken from me and mapping out what I was going to do with the rest of my life now it had been handed back to me.

I can say now that accident was the best thing that could

have happened to me. Life has not been sunshine and lollipops since then, and there are things in my life today that I wish were totally different, but still, that near-death experience gave me life.

Maybe you have experienced something similar, some moment of awakening or some shock that got you thinking differently. Or maybe you don't need one. What I hope to do in this book is to take some of my own clarity, my own perspective on my own life, mix it in with my 25 years' experience of helping clients use their money to live the life they want, and then add to it the financial planning knowledge I have to provide you with the right balance between life and money so you can build a financial plan that has your money supporting the life you want to live.

What life do you want to live?

This is a question that, strangely enough, very few people ask themselves anywhere near frequently enough. But it is also a question that very few people can actually answer.

Take a minute and ask yourself what you want the rest of your life to look like. What is important to you? What are your goals, values and objectives?

You really need to consider this. You need to be true to yourself. In this book I'll give you the steps to build a financial plan for yourself, but that plan will lack substance if it is not built around your goals, your values and your objectives.

When I first became a financial adviser, before I was a

financial planner, when I met a client for the first time I would look at their finances and build a financial plan for them. But the financial plan wasn't actually for them – it was for their finances. I would tell them what they needed to do with their money in order to get the most from it. The strange thing about doing it that way is that if somebody came in tomorrow with the same finances as the person I am meeting today they would both be getting the same financial plan. That makes no sense. How can the same financial plan cater for two different people?

It was around 20 years ago that I accepted that I wasn't really happy in my job. That's all it had become, a job. It took me some time but I realised all I was doing was fixing money problems. I wasn't actually fixing or helping people.

Maybe it is because my mother is a therapist and when I was growing up I saw the positive impact she had on people, helping them at their worst time. She made a difference to people. She didn't make their money grow, or change their pensions; she helped them. She helped them change things they weren't happy with. She helped them deal with past traumas or get out of current ones. She helped people.

Or maybe it is because of my dad. When I was two my dad had a heart attack, and he had a quadruple bypass. When I was six he had another heart attack and had three stents fitted. When I was eight he had another heart attack and had a quintuple bypass (that's five!). At that point Dad was only 48. He said to his doctor, 'In the last six years I have had three major heart incidents. What am I doing wrong?'

To which the doctor replied: 'There are two things, Micheal. One is you have sticky blood. It's hereditary, but you look after yourself. You drink very little, you cycle to work, you're not overweight. You can't really ask much more of yourself. The second thing is stress. What is the most stressful thing in your life?'

Dad sat back and thought about it for a while before saying 'Probably work'.

To which the doctor replied, 'Could you afford to give up work?'

Dad wasn't expecting this question and didn't know if he could. But he also wasn't sure if he wanted to: he was 48 years old, he had a good career and he was successful. Did he want to give up work? He decided to find out whether he could afford to and maybe that would help his decision process.

Dad had nothing to do with financial services or financial planning. But at some point along the way he had engaged with someone I would call an insurance salesman (it was the 1980s, so I will leave the 'man' there). The salesman had sold him an income protection policy. This meant that if his doctor and the insurance company's doctor agreed that Dad could not work on medical grounds they would pay him an income. In his case it was 66% of his current wage (it can be as high as 75% including social welfare benefits – it just depends on the policy you take out). They would pay him this income until either he was well enough to go back to work or he reached normal retirement age, whichever came first. It took Dad a while and maybe it was the acceptance that his medical situation was getting worse, not better, but at 50 Dad stopped working. That was in 1990. Dad died in 2020. I believe we got those extra years with Dad because he didn't have a financial crisis at the same time as a medical crisis.

I was ten when Dad gave up work to look after his health. I am not saying that at ten years of age I was screaming from the rooftops 'I want to sell income protection for the rest of my life', but when I finished college I was really attracted to financial services and ended up taking a job with Irish Life (which, by chance, was the same company paying Dad his income protection payment each month). I very quickly realised I wanted to help other families the same way that insurance salesman had helped ours.

I do believe that Dad's experience and his situation is the reason why I do what I do. But now I wonder if it's Mom and her profession that influenced me to change my approach to how I do it. Was it her influence that made me want to build financial plans based on people and what they want rather than being based purely on their money?

Whatever it was that drove me to make those changes 20 years ago, I now build financial plans with more meaning and purpose, and you should try to do this for yourself too. This book is going to show you the path to financial independence; it is going to give you a step-by-step guide to getting there. But believe me, it is all just a process. If you don't take the time to really figure out what you want from life, the goal of the financial plan becomes just to make the money pot bigger. That might sound great, but experience shows me that if making the pot bigger becomes your goal, you are on a neverending path of dissatisfaction. A path where your goal can never be achieved. A path where you will never realise how much is enough.

What are the things you want from life? At the very start of our financial planning process in Prosperous, the first time I get to meet clients I get to explore this very question. It is a fascinating process to take part in. Lots of people have big things they want to do in the future. Travel is often right up there near or at the top of the list. Sometimes people are incredibly detailed about their future travel plans. They might want to see new places and experience new things. Or they might want to go to sporting events – Augusta for the golf, or following the lads on a Six Nations tour. Sometimes it's all about food culture and some gastronomic adventure. Then there are the people who want to go on safari or see family in Australia or Canada or some other far-flung place. Others want one place: they dream of having a place in the sun or a house in the west of Ireland where they can retreat to.

Sometimes it is actually much more simple than that. I had one client who told me they didn't like taking time off work. They were in a high-powered executive role and they were very good at what they did. I asked them why they didn't like taking time off work, expecting them to say that it was because they ended up doing more work before they went away and then came back to find that all the work to be done while they were away was just sitting there waiting for them to come back. But even though this is probably exactly what happened, this wasn't actually their problem with taking time off work. They explained that what they liked doing when they were away from work was nothing. They were happy to stay at home and just read. Their problem was they felt uncomfortable when they went back to work and people asked them what they had done with their time off and they had to say 'Nothing'.

I think this is an important piece of the discovery journey you need to go on. Asking yourself what you want from life isn't about following societal norms. It isn't about what Disney tells us what life should look like. It is about you and what is important to you. This is your life – you decide.

It fascinates me that lots of us dedicate ourselves to our work, whether we're working for ourselves or for someone else. Between the ages of 40 and 65, assuming a five-day week and four weeks off a year, we will spend 52,000 hours, or about 25% of all the time we have, at work. Yet when I have these conversations with people it is very rare that somebody says, 'I want to work more, I love it.' Don't get me wrong – there are people who love their job, and I'm one of them. But I rarely, if ever, hear people say, 'Next year I want to work many more hours than I did this year.'

Interestingly, Harvard did some research that is somewhat related to this. They asked graduates of Columbia University whether their future priorities were money or time. Not surprisingly (well, not surprisingly for me, anyway), when they went back a year later and surveyed the same people they found that those chasing money were more likely to be less happy than those who prioritised time.

So ask yourself now: what makes you happy?

I find it interesting that we regularly get clients who have won the lotto, sold their business or come into money unexpectedly. I suppose when you suddenly have a large sum of money for the first time you don't have a professional network in your life to support that. You may be a little nervous about who to engage with and then you think, 'Sure there's your man off the telly; why not start with him?' and they reach out to me. Believe me, the privileged position I am in is not lost on me and we take the responsibility bestowed on us with pride, respect and responsibility. It really is a deadly position to be in and it feels amazing to be trusted by so many people.

When these clients come in for the first time one thing I try and explain to them is that if you're not happy already, this money isn't going to make you happy. The things that made you happy before are the same things that will make you happy now. The difference is you now have more time to do them. That's because now you have this money you can work less, or maybe you don't have to work at all, which gives you more time.

Having money does mean you can buy nice things. Having nice things might make you more comfortable, or look better, or even feel better. But will it make you happier?

When I think about things in the past, events from, say, five or ten years ago, what I remember are experiences. But they are experiences with people. For example, I won a trip to Italy to watch Leinster play in Parma. It was for two people and we would be flying on the same plane as the Leinster team.

I brought my son, who would have been about 12 at the time. I remember the trip so well. I remember the pizza we ate on plastic garden chairs in a restaurant in Rome called Montecarlo. I remember walking around a corner and seeing the Colosseum for the first time; more important, I remember Darragh's face as he saw it too. I remember spending hours throwing branches in the river and watching as they progressed down the rapids. I remember the train ride from Parma to Rome and Darragh's fascination that the train was going at 249 kph. I remember us going for a run together through the streets of Rome and him saying, 'Wow, every corner we run around there is something else to see.' I remember the time we spent together. I remember how it made me feel.

Do you know what I can't remember? I can't remember what phone I had at the time, or what clothes I bought. At a push I could probably guess what car I was driving, but that's only by working out which series of *How to be Good with Money* we were on and doing the calculation that way.

The point is that I vividly remember the experience, exactly how I felt on that trip and all the emotion that came with it, but – guess what? – I don't remember the things.

If my experience holds true for the past, why do we think the future is going to be any different? If we are buying some material object because we want it, because we know it will bring us happiness, great. But if we are buying it to satisfy societal pressures or because it is the thing to have or because everyone has one, ask yourself: In ten years' time, will I remember I had this now?

Engaging with a lotto winner isn't exactly as you might expect it to be. Yes, they are delighted and they're also a bit dazed, but what people are often surprised to hear is that lotto winners can also feel a level of sadness. And with that sadness comes a degree of guilt for being sad. 'How can I be sad when I have all this money?' When you think about it a little, they are grieving the life they once had. Their life is different now, and for ever. Different better? Most likely, if they navigate this new-found wealth properly. But it is different, and life will never be the same again. And they now have an added pressure. They have just been handed the opportunity of a lifetime. This money, if there's a lot of it, can change their lives for ever and can often change the lives of the people around them too. They are now, all of sudden, financially privileged. But with this comes the burden of pressure not to mess it all up. Yes, having €250 million can make you extremely happy. But, believe me, if you start with very little savings, get €250 million and waste it all, you are going to be exponentially more disappointed when you go back to having very little savings again than you would have been had you never won the money at all. So the sadness is more understandable when we look at it in this context; there is a brand-new burden of responsibility on the winner not to mess this up.

We also have to consider the other pressures. For example, if you win €250 million do you go public? If you do, handling the begging letters is one thing, but think of the dilemma that you face handling all the people in your life – all the family, friends and long-lost acquaintances who suddenly reappear. You start to question the motives of anyone new in your life and you can even become paranoid about whether bumping into your old school-mate on the street was a coincidence or if they set it up. Trying to decide who you are *not* going to gift money to may seem like your biggest problem. But it goes beyond that. Once you have decided to give money to somebody, knowing how much to give them is a nightmare. When you have €250 million and you give somebody €1 million, don't be surprised if the reaction is 'Is that all you think of me, is that the value you place on our relationship?' Even if this isn't their reaction it is still hard to keep the thought that this is exactly their reaction out of your mind.

The other issue lotto winners face is that they now have to really consider what their future looks like. In private practice, when I meet people who are working away, doing well, but unfortunately haven't won the lotto, in our first meeting we talk about what they see their future looking like. What things they want to do, places they want to see and experiences they want to have. We map it out together and at each successive annual review oftentimes things change, desires, goals and objectives become different. The point is they have time between now and their future. This time allows them to map it out, change it, but most important, think about it. For a lotto winner, all of a sudden their future is now today. For years, they have been working towards a retirement and adjusting their thoughts about what it would look like and now, overnight, they are retired. It also means that the future retirement you often thought about, the day when you reach financial independence, is now. Today. The future is now.

One key message we try and convey the first time we meet a lotto winner is that the things that made you happy in the past are the things that will make you happy in the future – you just have more time to do them. More time because you no longer have to work if you don't want to. You don't have to cut the grass, paint the fence or even cook your own dinner if you don't want to. Money buys you time because you can pay others to do things for you, and oftentimes these people do these things better than you would yourself because, as Roy Keane would say, 'That's their job.' Mix all those elements together, plus the fear that you might blow this money and the burden that you don't want to waste this opportunity, and all of a sudden you can see why people who win the lotto can be dazed and a little sad.

Having said all that, I would be more than willing to try to be happy with €250 million in my pocket – it would certainly be easier than the alternative!

Personally, I take on about 50 new clients a year. Each of them goes through a three-stage process. Later in this book I will take you through this process step by step. But each client goes through stage one, which includes what we call our 'first meeting'. This is where we have conversations about what retirement is going to look like. What people say about their hopes and dreams fascinates me. Often the person hasn't thought about this stuff in any sort of detail before. It is not unusual when we are talking to a couple for one to turn to the other and say, 'Do you really want to do that? I didn't know that.' It is also not uncommon for there to be tears. The process stirs up thoughts, emotions and aspirations and this can be emotional. That's okay. Most of us go through life without taking a step back and thinking about the whole purpose of this 'life thing'. Unless we crack our skull in three places, that is. So when we do it can affect people in different ways.

The process we go through is aimed to really get to the nub of what is important to people, to ask probing and stirring questions. Then I shut up and create the space for the person's mind to wander and the thoughts to emerge.

There are four key components in this initial discussion, and I'm going to ask you the same questions now.

I want you to imagine you are 75 years of age today and you are having a conversation with a loved one. (I'm not saying that at 75 your life is anywhere near over – there is still plenty of hill left to get over – but it is a good time to pause and reflect on life.) Imagine the loved one you are talking to asks you, 'Do you have any regrets? Are there things you thought you would get to do? Places you expected to visit or revisit? Or experiences you expected to have that you haven't had yet? What about achievements? What are you proudest of and what do you regret not achieving?'

The idea of this question is to make you reflective about what is actually your future. A bank manager once said to me, 'I have never seen a bad set of projections.' I agree with him. You see, we all imagine the future is going to be bright and all the things we want to do will happen someday. Most people imagine a future where they get to do all the stuff they want to do and achieve all the things they want to. We just think 'I'll do it someday.' Except in situations where people are going through a tough time mentally, we are pre-wired to imagine a positive future.

This is built into us as humans. Going way back in time, we had to be positive about the future. If we weren't positive and something bad happened, like a crop failure, why would we try again? The term 'optimism bias' describes what I am referring to. Basically, the fact that, unlike animals, we can imagine tomorrow, next week or even 20 years from now means we have the ability to plan but also to do things today that benefit our future selves. It is how or, probably more accurately, why we evolved.

Credit card companies play into this optimism bias. People are happy to put money on their credit card at ridiculous interest rates because the future is bright. 'Sure I'll clear it with the bonus that I will (or may not!) get next month.' If you question whether optimism bias exists, here's a little test to try the theory. Next time you are in a room with more than a handful of people who drive, ask them, 'Which of you is an under-average driver?'

Although optimism bias exists we do have to be careful because not all future thoughts are treated equally. One of my frustrations with the pension providers in Ireland is the fact that they use pictures of older retired people to sell their pensions. In one ad there are commuters standing on a train station platform looking miserable, trying to make their way to work. Then the camera pans out and reveals behind the station walls a couple in swimming gear, hats and all, jumping off a pier into the sea. The message is clear – this is what your retirement could look like if you buy one of our pensions. But they missed something in this ad campaign. People don't see others as themselves and therefore it is hard to resonate with that image, but, more interestingly, people don't even see their future selves as themselves. Let me explain.

This is my recollection of a piece of research I came across a long time ago, and I may not have remembered the finer details, but even if my recollection is questionable I do find the outcome logical, so let's go with it.

The researchers put people through a series of tests and monitored their brain activity. They checked what part of a person's brain lit up when they were asked different questions. What they found was if a person was asked about themselves, the X part of their brain lit up. If they were asked about somebody else, the Y part of their brain lit up. But if they were asked to think about themselves in the future, the Y part of their brain lit up. In other words, our brains think future us is somebody different.

What I am attempting to do with my looking back at 75 question is to break down both these barriers by asking you to be reflective and look at your life in the rear-view mirror. It is intended to reduce the impact of optimism bias. Asking you to imagine a conversation with a loved one is an attempt to create an emotional connection with future you. You see, your brain already loves the loved one you are imagining, so that emotion breaks down some of the barriers and helps you think more clearly about your future self as actually being you.

At that first meeting I have to prepare my clients for what's to come. My prep work doesn't always land; I might miss the mark or the client and I just don't immediately connect. Then I start to ask people to think about themselves at 75 looking back on their life and they look at me blankly and say, 'I thought we were going to talk about pensions!' I explain we will get to that but right now this is more important, and we try to keep going. We do always get there in the end, and it can be magical. You see people start to think deeply about what they want from life, the stuff that's important to them, and they begin to imagine all the things they will achieve and be proud of when they are 75 and looking back.

A lot of similar things come up. For some people travel is high on the agenda; for others enjoying home is important. Some people describe what they will achieve in their career or want to be proud that they got to retire early. For some it's about getting to attend the Masters or go on a Lions tour or being in Croke Park on All Ireland final day.

A common theme among high-level executives is that they want to look back at 75 and be proud of what they achieved in their second job. It is not unusual for people who work in a fast-paced, driven, pressurised environment to want to do something different once they step away from their current role. For example, someone in their early 50s and who is making a very healthy salary might have a burning desire to build a financial plan that enables them to step back from their current role at the age of 55 or 60 and earn a much lower salary to do something they are very passionate about or they feel they can make a difference in. This might be working for a charity or using the skill set they have to help others. One plan I heard recently, for the first time ever, was from a client who earns a very good salary but wants to be able to step away and become a librarian. It's just something he would love to do.

I get it. I have often gone through the toll bridge and looked at the person in the booth and thought what a brilliant job to have. You turn up to work each day, you do your job, and when you go home in the evening you don't bring any work problems home with you. You literally get to switch off every time you clock out. But maybe that's more a reflection of my inner thoughts than a desire to work in a toll booth. But a high-level executive's driver is often quite deep. Some of them feel that all their efforts simply make the big wheel turn just a little bit more smoothly. Sometimes they lack a real sense of meaning and purpose and they know that there must be more to it than this. In client meetings I am very conscious of this and I try to spot the signs early on. What I look for in all clients, whether they are senior executives, self-employed company owners or simply dedicated to their job, is signs that they are fulfilled by their role. Do they love it? Ultimately, the purpose of work is to generate the income to support the life we want. We don't have to love our job, but it makes life easier if it's fulfilling for us.

I have a theory that may offend some people. I don't believe you can suffer burnout if you are doing something you are truly passionate about. If you believe in what you are doing and, more important, if you feel what you are doing is making a difference to others it can be fulfilling, rejuvenating and satisfying. I am not saying you can't become physically tired, but to me burnout is something bigger – it's physical and mental exhaustion.

I believe if you don't find personal fulfilment in what you are doing it will very quickly burn you out. But the opposite is also the case: if you find something satisfying you will be enthusiastic, energised and able to stick with it much longer before becoming exhausted. Interestingly, something that once brought you fulfilment can become unfulfilling; equally, the person next to you may get fulfilment from doing exactly what you are doing. My point is, oftentimes it isn't the role itself but the headspace you are currently in or where your life is at that can determine whether something is fulfilling or not. Often it's an external factor that influences your feelings about your role. Maybe you have started to get fulfilment from other things in life and this has given you a different perspective; perhaps a life event has altered your goals and priorities. There can be lots of different factors, but it is important to recognise the signs sooner rather than later.

Let me give you an example from the sports world. (I should point out that this is my opinion, and I am far from qualified to give it; and I don't have any inside knowledge that isn't outlined in what I am about to write.) I recently had the privilege of interviewing the Dublin football legend Brian Fenton. Brian recently retired from inter-county football, when some would say he had several great years left in him.

There were lots of rumours about why he retired circulating at the time, but when I sat down to speak to him I came to my own conclusion. Brian is an amazing guy who oozes positivity and within minutes of meeting him you can see that he has an infectiously optimistic attitude about the world around him. From my experience of Brian I can honestly say I don't think that lad has a bad bone in his body.

When we talked about his later playing years I got a little insight into the early stages of fatigue for Brian. He had an impeccable disciplinary record while playing for the Dubs; in fact during his ten years playing at the highest level he only ever received one red card – he over-reacted to a situation that in previous years he would have simply brushed off. Interestingly, that was in the last year of his career. Personally, I think he was carrying a little frustration and I am guessing that part of that frustration was because he wasn't getting the same level of fulfilment he once had. When I asked him about the card he said maybe it was a sign that his time was coming to an end. Talking specifically about his decision to retire, he said there was no one big thing that led to his decision, but he did say that in previous years with the Dubs he would rush home from work, grab the gear bag, and couldn't wait to hit the training ground. In his last year, however, he was finding it harder to reach the same levels of enthusiasm.

As a Dublin supporter I was devastated to see him go. It was a big loss for the Dubs and I think we could have had a few more good wins with him controlling the middle of the field. But I also consider Brian a buddy and as a buddy I think he made the right decision for him. Whether he realised it or not I think the signs were there and he acted on them.

Luckily for Brian, he had his job, his fiancée Katie and his dog to go home to once the football stopped. We mere mortals often have a very different transition. Sometimes we don't recognise the physical and mental exhaustion we are going through until one day our body shuts down and we get sick. Other times we are forced out of a job because we reach 'normal' retirement age and because we have been around for some arbitrary 66 years all of a sudden we are no longer beneficial to our organisation.

The reality is that moving from working every day to not working is an incredibly difficult transition. When my clients go through the looking back at 75 exercise their mind often wanders to the thought of what their retirement is going to look like. For many it is important to have financial security; others talk about the golf they will play or the books they will read. Others mention all the free time they will have to spend with family and friends.

Having gone through the process with literally hundreds of clients, I know that the thought of retirement and the reality of retirement are two very different things. It is not always a smooth transition and some people go through a very rough time, particularly in the early part of their retirement. Think about it: you work for a company for 40 years, you put in the hard graft, you make a difference. Then you leave and three weeks later you realise that nobody is ringing you for guidance on how to fix things, the place is not falling down and the wheels just keep turning … without any help from you. What was the point of the long hours in the office, the sleepless nights and the sacrifices you made if after you walk away they are fine without you? Maybe that's why the toll booth job is attractive, because you know all this will happen without you and therefore there are no surprises when you stop.

Although everyone who retires goes through the transition of working to not working, not everyone has a tough time. But the ones who find it smoothest are the ones who are well prepared. You see, being retirement-ready is just as much about being prepared financially as it is about being prepared mentally. If you have not already retired, the day to prepare for retirement is today.

So how do you do it? There are two things you need to do. First, you need to be fully aware of what retirement actually looks like. Observe people in your life who are no longer working: what does their life look like? Does it look as if it would suit you? You might have an idea of beaches and bars, but their reality might show you that it just may not be your scene at that stage in life. More important than observing them, you should talk to them. Ask them what it's like, ask them how it is different from what they expected. Ask them if they'd do the same again and what they would do differently if they were where you are now.

Second, you need to practise retirement. That means exploring all the non-work things in life that excite you, entertain you and fulfil you. People who have a decent work-life balance and are tuned in to what is important to them will find this idea alien because, whether consciously or sub-consciously, they have been practising retirement already. Practising retirement is about doing the things you do when you have nothing else to do. I had a buddy once who was single, had a flexible job, and basically his time was his own. When I'd ask him what he was doing over the weekend his answer would be 'Whatever I want, whenever I want'.

Although practising retirement can be done in the evenings and at weekends, you also have to push yourself sometimes. When you take a two-week holiday, instead of jumping on the plane the day you finish work, then heading straight back to work the minute you get back, consider doing something different. What if you went away for one week and spent the other week at home? I don't mean being at home doing the big jobs around the house you never have time to do, I mean just doing ordinary life without the need to go to work. How often do we do this?

There are several advantages to this. First, let's focus on the financial one. Although a one-week holiday isn't 50% cheaper than a two-week one, it's still cheaper. Then, if you spend the second week at home you're not spending money on commuting. Looking beyond finance, and more interesting, is the research by Dr Tali Sharot that suggests that our peak enjoyment of holidays comes 43 hours into the trip. This could be because once we've unpacked and we're more or less settled in, we identify lots of things we want to do, we have the excitement of anticipating doing these things and we also have lots of time left to enjoy our holiday. We've also had lots of our 'firsts': our first dip in the pool, our first drink, our first meal, our first run ... It isn't that our second dip in the pool isn't enjoyable, it's just that it doesn't hit the same as the first. So If you lean into this research you might come to the conclusion that maybe a one-week holiday is as fulfilling as a two-week one. Maybe taking more one-week holidays would be more satisfying, rejuvenating and full of more firsts than fewer two-week holidays. But you also get the added benefit of being able to practise retirement in the second week.

Practising retirement with the second week of your long break from work each year is really useful, but you can step it up a level. We often do this with people who own and run their own business, but you would be surprised how many PAYE workers raise this with their employer, and it works out for them too. Consider the idea of a long break from work. I'm talking six, eight or even twelve weeks off. Now when I say this to the dedicated business owner they are aghast at the idea: 'There's no way I can take six weeks off work – the place would fall apart, I would have nothing to come back to.'

From a business perspective, if this is your reaction then this is exactly the reason why you should take a long break. If you're forced to take a break, for example through illness, or, like me, having had brain surgery and worrying if the business will be there when you get better, I guarantee you will find it a lot more comfortable lying in that bed if you have previously tested how the business would survive without you in it for a prolonged period of time. Interestingly, the reason big corporations often say yes to people requesting extended leave is for a very similar reason; you not being available tests the organisational chart and often results in the business become stronger. It is much clearer in a small business, where the impact is often easily recognised, but it is true of large multinational corporations too.

The other advantage businesses get from owners or employees taking extended leave is it is often in this period that the superstars in waiting show their true colours. The void is created because you are not in the business and somebody, often somebody unexpected, steps in to fill that void so the business continues to move forward.

If you are thinking 'There's no way my boss would give me extended leave' you need to be clever in how you go about it and you need to make it easier for them. Don't tell them you want to do it next week; say you want to do it in 18 months' time. This shows you are committed to the business for at least the next 18 months, it shows you care about coming back – if you didn't you'd just hand in your notice in 17 months' time – and it shows you have the ability to think strategically. Explain to them how it would benefit the business and how it would be good for Johnny or Mary to temporarily step up and the business will be able to test them without a long-term commitment to them staying in that role.

But, and this is important, once you have them onside you need to tell them about how good it is going to be for you. Explain that you will come back with a full battery, you will be rejuvenated and ready to hit the challenges the business faces. You will have time to get yourself out of the trenches and really think about the improvements you can make in your role and for the business. It will give you clarity of thought. Another reason why your boss may want to get this signed off is that if you sell the personal benefits to you they'll start to think, 'I wouldn't mind a piece of that for myself' and are more likely to push it with whoever else needs to be convinced in the hope that they too can do the same. Whether you are asking your boss or you are the boss, the benefits to you and your business are the same. As the boss, ask yourself if a key member of staff asked for this break, what would you say? Why? And then ask yourself, are you a key member of staff?

Once you have sign-off for an extended break from work, the first priority is to make sure it works smoothly for the business. You don't want to mess things up for other people and you do want to be able to do this again. Put the groundwork in, train the people who will cover for you. If there are big tasks that can be done before you go, get them done.

You also need to start preparing yourself. Are you financially prepared? Will you be paid or is this all unpaid leave? What financial changes can you make to make sure that you don't spend a second of your time off worrying about money? If you are going to be gone for a while, have you a mate or relative who could rent your house short term? Can you suspend some of your subscriptions or gym memberships? Think of the practical things that you won't need if you are away and, without causing heartache for yourself, see if you can eliminate some costs.

Next comes the actual planning of your leave. At this point

we need to remind ourselves of the purpose of this exercise – at its core this is about you practising retirement. By all means take a long break if that's what's important to you, but you also need to plan some dull time, time when you are just at home with no plans. You need to create the space for your true interests, hobbies and loves to flow into and you can truly find out what it is that brings you happiness and contentment.

I have had many clients do this mini-retirement over the years and it is truly remarkable what they report back afterwards. Some talk about really enjoying the dull time with nothing to do and others decide they never want to give up work! But all report how much of a leveller it is. It gives you clarity on what you want to do. But it also reminds you what it is you are striving towards, why you bother getting out of bed in the morning at all, what it's all for. (I also live in hope that Brian Fenton is actually just on a mini-retirement from the Dublin panel and will come back rejuvenated!)

The looking back at 75 exercise and the extended holidays are all aiming in the same direction. You are trying to figure out what it is that is important to you, what gives you joy and what you find fulfilling.

When we make these questions more immediate we often find we have different priorities. My good friend Clare, who had cancer and who died ten years ago, had a way of making you think about the here and now. She asked me to ask my clients the two-year question: if you had your full health for the next two years and then you were going to die, what would you do with the next two years? Forget about money, assume that's sorted. What things are you going to do more of? And what things will you strip out of your life for the next two years? Interestingly, in my experience, about 50% of people say they will keep working; lots of people talk about travel; others talk about some of the things they mention when I ask the 75 looking back question. What is most fascinating for me is the difference in the answers. But something like career progression or getting a promotion, which used to seem important, is insignificant when you put it in the perspective of life being over in two years' time.

A question I have been using more recently, morbid as it is, has been very powerful. I was stirred to ask this question based on two things I learned. The first isn't backed up by any actual research; the second is based on a piece of research by Donald R. Nichols and Ernest L. Zweig.

The first thing that stirred up my thinking was that only four people will cry at your funeral. Now, I can't imagine a researcher standing at the back of your funeral, clipboard in hand, asking the mourners 'Did you cry?', so we will take it as anecdotal. But it is stark all the same. If only four people will cry at our funeral, why do we worry so much about what other people think of us? Why do we go out of our way to please others? Wouldn't it be great if we could identify those four people now and then just concentrate our energy on them? I am not saying others aren't upset and I am not trying to encourage you to remove people who bring you joy from your life. What I am hoping this information does is concentrate your mind a little and help you focus not just on what is important to you but also who is important. I am hoping it helps you identify who the inner circle is, because the research by Nichols and Zweig widens the net a little.

Their research, entitled 'Weather to go?', looked at the impact the weather has on attendance at funerals. They found that bad weather could reduce the attendance at a funeral by as much as 50%. Imagine that somebody knows you well enough to consider going to your funeral but a bit of rain ultimately makes them decide you weren't important enough to them.

During lockdown a lot of things were taken from us, including the ability to meet up with people whenever we wanted to. There's no doubt there were people we missed so much it was painful. But there was also a group of people who were no longer able to be in your life who I bet you didn't miss. Ask yourself these questions now. How many of those people were there? Who are they? Have you since let them back into your life? And, if so, why?

Now, more importantly, focus on the people you missed. Appreciate the fact that you can now see them whenever you want. Cherish those relationships that mean something to you because, ultimately, this is what is important.

Harvard have been doing a study for more than 85 years. In 1938 they started following the lives of 724 men, and they still follow those who are still alive. Initially they didn't believe that relationships could have an impact on our physical health. That was until the accumulated evidence couldn't be ignored. Not only have they come to the conclusion that loneliness kills, they have found loneliness is as dangerous as smoking or alcoholism. They have also found the opposite to be the case too. People who had strong relationships had significantly lower rates of chronic diseases including cardiovascular disease and diabetes, and they also had better physical and mental health. It is important to note that the study finds that it is not the quantity of the relationships people have but the quality that's important.

This study is one of the most fascinating pieces of research I have ever come across. You see, I truly believe that life is about experiences, not things. But this study has pushed my thinking even further – life is in fact about people. I would argue that it is the enjoyment of experiences with people you love and hold close that further enhances our relationships and thus makes us all happier. And, it seems, it even makes us healthier.

Of course money is important, but only as a vehicle to facilitate your ability to nurture, cherish and enjoy the people you hold closest in life. It is only through this lens that you actually start to understand what is important to you. It is only when you truly understand that it's people, not things, that are important that you get real clarity on what you want in your future. Only then can you truly start to build a proper financial plan that is true to your goals, your values, your objectives. It is only then that you can build a real financial plan.

Where do you start?

Guess what? You have already started. As you have probably gathered by now, I recognise that money is important, but it is not as important as experiences and the people we surround ourselves with. But we do have to be good with money. Time and time again, in polls about what people's biggest stressors are, money comes up in the top three things that keep us awake at night. So we need to learn how to control it instead of it controlling us. In this section we are going to look at several different areas. We will look at the big mistakes we make with our money, the pitfalls and the traps we can fall into that can set us back weeks, months and sometimes even years.

I also want to explore the outside influences that cause us, sometimes unknowingly, to take actions and make decisions in our day-to-day lives that we may not want to take. This is where we will look at biases and heuristics.

The big mistakes

In general, I try to have a positive look on life, and I always try to see the bright side of even the worst situations. Don't get me wrong, I am far from perfect, but I do believe that no matter how bad a situation is there is always a positive side to it.

One of those moments I had was sitting at the end of my friend Clare's bed. I mentioned Clare earlier – she was diagnosed with cancer at 30 years of age and at the time of writing she has been dead just over ten years. But the moment that jumps to mind is the discussion I was having with her that day. We were, for the first time, talking about the fact that she was going to die. I got upset and she sternly told me 'Eoin, you are just selfish.'

Here I was, in tears because she was going to die, and here she was, putting me in my place and putting perspective on things for me. She said that she was at peace that she was going to die – it wasn't that she wasn't sad, it was just she had come to accept it. She also said that she had really enjoyed her life. At that moment I really noticed she had this really strong, powerful calm about her and a hyper-clarity about what was important. Despite all that was going on, it was what she said next that really gave me the awakening I needed. She said, 'I am in pain, I want the pain to stop, I will be gone. When I'm gone I won't feel the sadness but I won't feel the pain either. You are only sad because of how you will feel after, but you are not thinking about me, you are thinking about you.'

At a moment that was incredibly difficult for me, Clare gave me a different perspective on it all. This perspective has helped me with so many difficult situations in my life since. My dad spent the best part of six months in hospital before he died, and as I watched him deteriorate I remembered what Clare had said. I reminded myself that I was being selfish. Don't get me wrong, I was in a heap. But Clare's words gave me the strength I needed to think of it from Dad's perspective. It helped me to accept his time had come. It even helped me enjoy the last few months I had with him instead of being angry with the circumstances.

You see, I think every situation has a positive side. You may not be able to see it today, but at some point you will look back and say 'That happened because …'

Take redundancy, for example. When it happens to you

it feels as if the world has come tumbling down. Even in situations like a global pandemic or the global financial crisis, when something that is completely out of your control results in you being made redundant, you still feel that somehow you are to blame. For some, this is a fleeting thought; for others, it scratches away at them and can even make them question their value in the workplace. I have seen people in absolute turmoil due to redundancy. I have seen it stop families in their tracks for weeks and start a grieving-type process for the person affected and those around them.

Part of the reason for those awful feelings is the loss of control. You go from having a steady wage coming in each week or month to not knowing when your next pay cheque will be. It can be debilitating and scary. But it can also leave you with a sense of not being in control of your financial destiny.

Despite the awful experience of going through a redundancy I have yet to meet a person who was made redundant who, within six to twelve months, did not reflect on the entire thing and say, 'It's the best thing that ever happened.' This is usually because they have found a better job or a better position, or because they are doing something now that they would never have taken the leap to do if they hadn't been pushed.

To me that's another example of a horrendous situation having a silver lining. No matter how crap things are, no matter how bad they get, I still think there is something positive to be found in the vast majority of situations and I think we are all better served thinking positively than negatively.

Now, I can hear the naysayers shouting, 'Positive thinking

isn't magic dust!' I understand that; it's easy to believe that you can't think yourself out of a bad situation. But let's consider the alternative.

Let's think about the economy for a minute. Every three to five years we have what the media might call a stock market crash, but what I prefer to call a temporary decline – they are a decline and they are temporary. If we go back over the last number of years we can see a pattern: Covid, Brexit, Trump 1, the global financial crisis, the dotcom bubble, the Russian crisis, the Asian crisis, black Monday … we're now back to the late 1980s and all these were roughly three to five years apart.

The reasons for these 'crashes' are often, but not always, quite different, but their patterns and outcomes are often very similar. For example, 80% of stock market crashes fully recover within three years.

> We will get into investing later, but if the outcome of these events is typically the same (i.e. 80% of them fully recover within three years), what do you think is the best thing to do? Let me tell you: the best thing to do when your pension or investments are in one of these declines is nothing. Invest and forget. With one exception: if you have any cash, get it invested, because statistically the good days come after the bad ones.

These market events are simply cyclical, a rest period, if you like. I don't think anyone would disagree with me if I said that stock markets overreact, they overreact on the positive and they overreact on the negative. So these readjustments every few years is simply a reset, but even in a reset they overreact, resulting in brilliant years of performance following the crash. In fact, between 1926 and 2022 US stock markets were on average up 41.1% after three years following a 20% crash.

These cycles will continue and they usually accompany a recession. Every time I am asked 'Do you think there's a recession coming?' my answer is always yes, because as winter follows autumn, there is always one coming.

Let's imagine we are in one right now. Do you think it is possible that if we started to think negatively it might get worse? If the entire country believes the news headlines that this time is different, the world has changed for ever, it has never been this bad before, it is going to get worse, we will never recover from this, then the entire nation will start to behave as if it were true. The negative thinking will result in less spending by individuals. Sales will fall, VAT take will go down and businesses will be under pressure. Lower sales means that people will lose their jobs, resulting in less income tax coming in and more social welfare payments going out. Companies will not only have to let staff go, they will also have to halt or cancel plans to expand or invest. Capital expenditure will go down, the economy will slow further and it could result in an economic spiral that is self-perpetuating.

Although in general I believe it to be true that positive thinking makes things better, I can see how others can hold an opposite view that you can't 'positive think' your way out of a bad situation. I often come across these people – strangely enough, the more positive you are yourself the more likely you are to be challenged by people who believe the opposite. These people often agree that, as in the example of a spiralling economy, you can make things worse by thinking negatively, but they often struggle to accept that you can make things better by thinking positively. Surely if you believe one to be true you can't ignore the other.

I also find that certain people hold more influence and therefore have more responsibility when it comes to offering an opinion on things being positive or negative. It is easy to recognise that people often hang on politicians' every word, particularly at a time of crisis. When they say something, especially if it is negative, it gets amplified and repeated. When they say something positive the people who want to hear the positive will hear it, but the people who are seeking out a negative will always find some fault in what is being said.

But it goes far beyond the politicians. When I am presenting in a corporate environment I often remind the audience of their own personal responsibility. If you are working in a big multinational and you are at the side of a football pitch at the weekend talking to a neighbour or somebody else and you talk negatively about the economy, for example, don't underestimate the weight of your comments. Think it through for a second. When someone repeats what you've said it can add weight to it, especially when they add 'and sure they would know – they work in XYZ multinational down the town'.

This brings its own level of personal responsibility on lots of people in society but there is nothing more important than the responsibility we have to ourselves.

Our thoughts, our mindset and how our attitude affects our daily lives is something that fascinates me. I am not an expert, but it is something I have spent a lot of time researching, and one of the most fascinating discoveries I have come across is the fact that our brain lies to us, all the time. Our brain will store information in a way that suits the narrative we have told ourselves to be true. A simple example of this is confirmation bias. If you believe a referee in a match is being unfair to your team you will notice and scrutinise every time the referee calls a free against them. But when you store that information in your brain it will be given more prominence each time the referee awards a free. After the match you will recall more bad calls than good ones. This is the brain's way of confirming you are right. Confirmation bias is a lie our brain tells us all the time. We like to be right and our brain finds ways to back us up, even when it means the brain has to lie to us.

It is the same with people and money. People often say to me 'Oh, I am very bad with money,' to which I reply 'Of course you are. That's because you keep telling yourself you are and your brain keeps finding ways to prove it.' Your brain is powerful, and it finds ways to confirm you are right, even to the extent of making decisions that simply make no financial sense.

Mo Gawdat goes into this in quite a lot of detail in his book *Solving for Happy*. It is a great book, in which he, as an engineer, tries to decipher whether there is an algorithm that could be used to create happiness. In the book he writes about the concept that we are not our brains; we are us and our brain is simply supporting 'us'. He explores the topic in depth and it literally messes with your brain when you start to think about your brain as a separate support function, just as your heart is a support function. It also begs the question, if we aren't our brain then what is 'us'? But I will let you read the book yourself to go on that path. My takeaway for now is that once you accept that your brain is not 'you', you can start to question what your brain tells you. You can start to critically analyse the information your brain provides. If you don't like what you're being told, push back and ask the brain to try again and try harder. The brilliance of this is that although, if you go along with the concept, your brain is not 'you', your brain is working for you. Your brain also wants to please and it also, as we saw in the football match example, wants to prove you right. So if you flick the switch and start asking your brain for positive things instead of negative ones it will literally start giving them to you to both make you happy and prove you right.

If you accept this concept, it is not a massive leap to the idea that we become what we tell ourselves to be, and our brain finds ways to get us there. Be careful about what you tell yourself you want to be or what you want to achieve. Try to be positive and even if a situation feels desperate, try to find the silver lining. In my experience there is always one, even if it takes weeks, months or even years to recognise it.

I am not saying we should go around all happy-clappy with our hands over our ears and ignoring anything negative; I am saying that where there is something negative we should take action to turn it into a positive. After all, there is no win or lose, there is only win or learn.

Now given the way I have teed this up I have made the next section much more challenging for myself. I am about to lay out all the bad or negative things people do with their money and then try to find not only a solution but a positive for you to take away from them, so after all the positive talk let's hit a bunch of negatives.

30 big mistakes

1. Trying to do too much in one go

I see it all the time. People come to a speech I am giving and they come up afterwards and tell me how enthused they are to get going. They tell me they have decided they are going to spend all of next weekend pulling apart their finances and putting them back together, just like I said in my talk. Over the course of one weekend they are going to become good with money.

What do you think is the inevitable outcome here? Ultimately they fail. They get stuck in, they get bored and they give up. Why? Because money is boring and so it should be. We should be getting our excitement and enjoyment out of life, not an Excel spreadsheet. When we jump in, all excited, the excitement dissipates very quickly and most sane people quickly give up.

It's not that we behave like a four-year-cld, putting a puss on our face, slumping in the kitchen chair and declaring 'I'm bored' – our brains are much kinder to us than that. What typically happens is that we get stuck in, subconsciously get bored and then our brain comes to the rescue and finds reasons why we can't continue. For example, you decide to find out if your pension is set up properly, with the correct funds and a competitive charging structure, but you quickly realise there is a lot to this. Then you start going down the Google rabbit hole to find out what is a good fund and how much you should be getting charged. Forty-five minutes pass and you realise that actually you have achieved nothing. You are more confused now than when you started and your brain looks for a way out. The narrative goes something like this:

> *Argh! I can't remember my password to get into my work pension, and the office is closed on Saturdays. It's not that I want to give up; after all, today is the day I am sorting my finances forever. Alas, this is out of my control. I'll get the password next week and fully tackle this next weekend.*

What happens next weekend? Nothing. It wasn't a great experience last weekend so you avoid going back to it. Yeah, you found out some stuff about random funds and how they work, but ultimately you didn't get anywhere. So why would you sign yourself up to do that again next weekend? Don't fool yourself – you don't say 'I am not doing that next weekend.' Instead you say to yourself 'I must get back to that,' and then find an excuse not to. There's nothing wrong with what you're trying to achieve here – it is the approach that isn't working.

I have run a few marathons. I like the training because you can't cheat. If you run regularly and clock up decent mileage each week you can with a small amount of effort sign up to a 10k or even a half marathon and wing it. You won't break any course records, but you will get through. But there is no hiding in a marathon; if you don't put in the training you will be found out on marathon day, and it hurts. At the time of writing I have run 11 marathons, but I am not an elite runner, not even one tiny bit. I have done a few sub-four-hour marathons, but most have been around the 4.00/4.20 mark. I have run two that took me more than five hours – Boston in 2025 and London in 2018. I had put in a very decent block of training for both, and if the conditions had been right I would have done both much better. But unfortunately for me they weren't. London that year was the hottest marathon recorded in its history; it was well over 20 degrees that day. The forecast for Boston was 11–13 degrees and cloudy, but it delivered blue skies and 18–20 degrees. I don't like heat, but remember in each case there were between 30,000 and 50,000 people out there with me in the same heat and not all of them underperformed as I did. Personally I think running a marathon in over five hours is exponentially more difficult than running a personal best marathon. When you run at your personal best level everything goes right, everything feels right and you glide. I am not saying it doesn't hurt – it does. It is just that you are expecting the pain and therefore you deal with it much better.

When I am running a marathon I break it down into three components: my head – am I feeling positive or negative right now?; my torso – how is my heart, how is my breathing, how does my body feel?; and my legs – can they keep moving, are they cramping, do they feel strong? When one component is struggling I concentrate on how good the other two are feeling; when two are struggling I really zone in on the one that feels good. When things are going well you swap to which one or two in that moment are feeling good and ignore the parts that are struggling. But when the wheels start to come off and your head, your torso and your legs are screaming at you it starts a spiral and it becomes painful to finish. Thankfully I've finished each marathon I started, but Boston in 2025 was the closest I have come to quitting. I sat in the medical tent at mile 22 (4.2 miles from the finish) and I really had a good chat with myself. I had never been in a medical tent during a race before and I realised whilst I was sitting there that other than the pain I was in there was actually nothing wrong with me. It was my brain giving up and begging me to stop. But then I reasoned with my brain that if I gave up the pain I would feel afterwards would be far greater than the pain I was feeling now. I knew Clara (my partner) was at the finish line – she had run it too – I knew my phone was broken and I knew the quickest way to get to Clara was to run, walk or crawl the last 4.2 miles. So that is what I did.

I can't express enough how much it was worth it. That finish line, meeting Clara after she finished her first ever marathon (despite struggling with an injury for six weeks before the start line she had still kicked my ass), the 30 minutes or so we sat on a kerb and said little or nothing to each other, the struggle to get to the Four Seasons on Boston Common, the struggle to walk to the bar once we found a seat, the cold glass of champagne we enjoyed and then the $38 Uber ride to go 700 metres. These were all part of a single day that will be a core memory for me for life. I don't think it would have been as memorable if everything had gone to plan. I don't think I would have appreciated finishing as much if I had not gone through the pain. I don't think it would have meant as much if I didn't know Clara was at the end.

Marathon training is hard – the early mornings, the aches and pains, the wind, the rain, the sunshine. But for me, it is worth it. What I love about marathon training is that nothing scares me like it. Looking forward to days like Boston is why you get out of bed at 5 a.m. on a Tuesday morning to get your run in.

If you don't put the work in you get found out by a marathon, and it is the same with money, specifically tackling your money. If you feel you are not on top of your money, setting aside a weekend to fix a lifetime of habits just won't cut it – you will be found out. A much better way of tackling it is to do it like you would train for a marathon. Do it in bite-sized chunks. With marathon training you do lots of short runs, long runs and speed sessions, and in the same way you should tackle your finances bit by bit. After all, if you don't run right now you are not going to set aside time next weekend to run a marathon.

The other trick to overcoming this problem is to give yourself a quick win. My suggestion is that the first time you do it, you set aside no more than 20 minutes to tackle your finances. But you need to do the prep work in order to maximise the time you have allocated.

A great place to start is your gas and/or electricity bill. The utility companies love how lazy people are. Most people, unless they are forced to, don't do anything about any of their utility bills, and these companies take advantage of this tardiness. They sit on the sideline shouting to new customers, telling them how shiny and new and attractive they are. They give new customers discounted rates and giveaways knowing full well that most people who sign up won't review their rates and options once the initial contract expires and they move to standard customer rates. People automatically roll over to the new, more expensive, rates and don't think about it again until years later, something over there looks shiny and new and the cycle begins again.

My suggestion is to start here. A few days before you sit down for your first 20-minute session, either download or print out your gas and/or electricity bill. Doing it a few days before, ideally during normal business hours, means that if there is an issue you can contact the provider.

When your 20 minutes comes round, sit down with your bills in hand and log on to cru.ie. CRU (the Commission for Regulation of Utilities) is a government agency that regulates the utility companies, and it also provides details on the three (or sometimes four) companies that are authorised to switch you from one provider to another.

These companies are in competition with each other so it is in their best interest to make the switch as smooth and as easy as possible. They get paid when you switch and they don't have a monopoly. All the details they need to provide you with a comparative quote are on your bill.

Switching typically takes a lot less than 20 minutes and it is very typical for somebody switching one provider to save about €300 and switching both gas and electricity to save around €500 per year.

When you get that win it feels good. It was relatively effortless and you feel that you are taking control of your finances. The temptation then is often to jump in again in search of your next quick win. Don't.

Like a good training run, you need to walk away feeling you had a lot more to give. The benefit of this far outweighs the risk you run of walking away tired, resulting in the entire session being a negative experience. When you get the quick win and the positive experience of saving money it is the opposite of what we talked about earlier; your brain will find ways to convince you to do it again. Remember, your brain does actually want you to feel good. What happens next is that your brain goes into stealth mode and over the next few days and weeks it will seek out other quick wins that will give you a feeling of control over your finances again. Maybe your home insurance, which you typically ignore and roll over, comes through the door and it now becomes your next challenge. A challenge you gladly accept because of the success you have just experienced with your gas/electricity.

But then you notice other things, like the personal finance segment on the radio, which you usually half listen to, suddenly becomes highly absorbing as you're in search of your next nugget of information that will lead to your next quick win.

This happens as a result of what's called the Baader-Meinhof phenomenon, or the frequency illusion. In simple terms, when our brain looks for something it finds it. Or, more precisely, it notices things that it previously dismissed as irrelevant. It is particularly relevant to learning a new skill, where information you previously had no interest in was discounted or ignored now becomes of interest to you and it feels like this information is everywhere. Let's say you buy a red car. Although there aren't all of a sudden more red cars on the road than there were before, your brain starts to notice the ones that are and that makes you feel like there are more red cars on the road.

Remember, you control your brain, it does not control you. So when you prime it with what you are looking for it will supply it, and often in truckloads. Your brain also wants to make you feel good so it seeks out the stuff that helps you achieve that goal. You get what you ask for, so be careful what you ask for.

Getting a quick win is a game-changer and has you on the road to starting to tackle your finances. You might be thinking you're well beyond this stage, and you may well be, but it does help to remind ourselves that we need to get the foundations right. If we don't and we create real wealth these foundations will crack and you will be on shaky footing.

> It is important that when you do identify savings you put them to work, whether that is to tackle debt, build a buffer or fund your pension. If you don't put them to work, lifestyle creep kicks in and your lifestyle expands to fill the income you have available. We will talk much more about this later on.

2. Taking on debt

Borrowing from the future to pay for today is basically putting yourself on a financial treadmill and wondering why you are tired all the time. Through my years presenting *How to be Good with Money* on RTÉ One, one of the things I became accustomed to was the number of applicants we got each year in their mid- to late twenties with a negative net worth.

These applicants found themselves on the financial back foot very early on in life because they borrowed money to pay for things like cars, holidays and sometimes even just nice clothes. While there were plenty of people who had student debt or had borrowed just to get by, for every one of them there were multiples of people who had simply accumulated debt because they could and they wanted to enjoy life today.

When we take out a loan we borrow from the future to pay for today. We literally get given a lump of money and we promise to pay it back out of income we haven't even earned yet.

What people often don't realise is that we live in a system that encourages this, but if we could shift our thinking a little bit we could end up in a much better position. Instead of thinking that the holiday loan you are taking out is paying for your holiday, think about the fact that the loan you are taking out is actually paying for your banker's holiday. The interest you pay fuels their profits, pays their salary (and bonuses) and ultimately pays for their holiday.

These bankers, who are often well intentioned, sell you the loan on the basis of immediate gratification. They sell it to you on the basis that they are doing you a favour. They aren't. You are doing them a favour – you are paying for their holiday. Even the idea that you 'might not get the loan' makes you feel differently, even privileged that you did. The entire system has been constructed around the idea that getting a loan is a good thing. You walk into a bank and they don't have picture of a person sitting at their kitchen table looking at their banking app, with their head in their hands, wondering how they will pay for bread and milk. They have pictures of white sandy beaches with blue waters crashing on them and a hammock in the corner. But the reality of a loan is closer to the kitchen table than it is sand between your toes.

Borrowing money is expensive, no matter how it is dressed up. Take two people, let's call them Salt and Pepper. Salt and Pepper are mates but they have very different ways of going about their finances. Silly Salt always tends to do the wrong thing and Proper Pepper (or Prosperous Pepper, after my firm, prosperous.ie) tends to do everything right.

In this instance Salt and Pepper are going on holiday together. They are both 20 and so they plan on backpacking to save money. They reckon the total cost of the holiday will be €600 and they are going in 12 months' time. Pepper starts saving €50 per month and after 12 months the holiday is paid for. Salt forgets to start saving and has to borrow the €600.

They both go away and they both really enjoy it. However, and if you have ever saved specifically for a holiday this will resonate with you, even though they both did the same things, Pepper actually enjoyed it a little more. That's because Pepper set a goal and achieved it and was very pleased to get their reward. But there is another element too, Pepper doesn't come home from the holiday with the financial hangover that Salt has, and, even more important, Pepper isn't facing 12 months of loan repayments.

Whatever about feeling better about not going into debt for a holiday, how does it work out financially over time? Let's assume that Salt's loan was €600 over 12 months at 10% interest.

The repayments would be €52.75 per month or €633 in total. Honestly, €33 in interest doesn't seem that bad. But let's imagine this happens every year for the next ten years – we'll go easy on Salt and assume the holiday was so good that they never spend more than €600 on a holiday again, but each time they clear a loan they take out another €600 to cover the cost of this year's holiday. In total they will borrow €6,000 and in total they will make repayments over the ten years of €6,330.

Now, €330 in interest for ten years of holiday memories doesn't seem too bad for someone who is Salt with their money, but it goes deeper. First you must consider the fact that 10%

interest isn't the worst rate out there; if Salt put the holiday on the credit card at a rate of 20%, now all of sudden the interest doubles. The repayments go from €52.75 to €55.58 per month and the total interest bill over ten years becomes €670.

But you also need to look at the opportunity cost. You see, when Pepper came home they realised that Salt had stuck the holiday on the credit card and asked them what the repayments were. Pepper then decided to do their €50 per month savings for their holiday next year but separately decided to 'invest' the difference between their savings and what Silly Salt had to make in loan repayments. Pepper is always trying to get one step ahead of Salt – that's just the way their brain is wired. At the end of the ten years Pepper won't just have enjoyed all their holidays interest free but, ignoring tax and assuming 6% growth, they would have accumulated €914 in savings just using the same amount of money that Salt was paying in interest.

Now, you might be thinking that if you do everything right you end up €250 better off, whoopee. But you don't, you end up €900 better off. Salt is at minus €670 and Pepper is at plus €914 – that's a swing of over €1,500.

In this example I've kept the numbers low to make them understandable and relatable. If you do exactly the same maths using 8% interest on a car loan of €50,000 the swing becomes a whopping €51,232.

> A loan of 50k at 8% over five years is €1,013.81 per month. Over five years the total repayments are €60,828.60. If we double that to make it comparable to the ten years we used above, total repayments become €121,657.20. This is €21,657.20 in interest.
>
> Saving €50,000 over five years at 0% growth would require a savings amount of €833.33 per month. This means Salt is paying €180.47 per month in interest. If Pepper were to save this per month at 6% growth, ignoring tax, after ten years they would have €29,575 in their investment.
>
> Salt spent €21,657.20 in interest, and Pepper saved €29,575, so the swing is €51,232.

But borrowing money goes well beyond the maths. When you save money and spend it the transaction takes up no head space once it's been done. In fact, people regularly report enjoying the thing they bought or experienced more because they 'did it right'.

In recent years we have seen the development of an even more frightening lending practice: buy now, pay later, or BNPL. We saw the first iterations of this mostly in furniture stores, where you're surrounded by signs that say 'Spread the cost over three monthly payments' and they also have '0% interest' plastered all over the signage.

BNPL has now developed even further and is offered on practically anything you want to buy. Recently I was ordering a takeaway and I was told I could split the cost (€40) over three equal payments at 0% interest. It was a takeaway!

The scary thing about this for me is recent research conducted by the CCPC (Competition and Consumer Protection Commission), which found that more than one in three people didn't see BNPL as a form of credit. That is scary. They did not believe a loan was a loan.

What's scary about it is where it could lead people to. I would hope when someone is taking out any loan they are doing it consciously and are aware that they are promising part of their future earnings for the set period of time to pay this loan back. But if you don't think it is even a loan then your guard is completely down, particularly if you combine that with the ridiculousness of the fact you can get a loan for a spice bag.

To me, BNPL is the modern-day version of payday loans. A payday loan is basically a loan facility often used by people in the awful position of finding that there's too much month left at the end of their money. In other words, they ran out of money before their next pay cheque. That's when the payday loan stepped in. They would borrow money that had to be paid back in full from their next pay cheque.

They were once incredibly popular in the US and were often facilitated in local payday loan stores that were set up in often disadvantaged areas across America. At one point they were so popular that there were actually more payday loan stores than there were McDonald's outlets in the US.

They haven't disappeared completely in the US, but a couple of factors have resulted in a dramatic decline of their use. First, the move by BNPL firms like these simply makes more commercial sense; they don't have to have a store and they can reach more customers at the point a purchasing decision is being made or the need for money arises.

Regulation has also had an impact. Many states have banned payday loans altogether and other states have put caps on the interest rates being charged, thus making the practice less attractive commercially.

One of the biggest issues with payday loans was that although interest rates were capped from a very early stage of the life cycle of the development of payday loans, many companies overcame this by using rollover loans, which is one of my biggest concerns with BNPL. A rollover loan meant that when you were due to pay the loan back but didn't have the money to pay it back, you would roll it over and take out a new loan to repay the original one. Your new loan would cover the initial amount of money you borrowed plus the interest you owed on that loan. Interest on interest. It all spiralled very quickly. Back in 2014, at the height of the payday loan era, studies found that 80% of payday loans were cleared using another payday loan, so only 1 in every 5 loans was cleared as expected.

The interest rate on some payday loans at one stage was recorded to be as high as 1,900% per annum. The differ-ence with BNPL is that the interest rate is often 0%. So A: What's the problem? And B: How do they make money?

Let's handle B first. A little research shows quite an interesting business model. Whenever you buy something in a shop using an ordinary credit or debit card the card issuer takes a cut of that sale. So if the thing you are buying is €100 your credit card company/bank would usually get €1 or €2. The retailer bears this cost as a convenience to you but also because they don't have to take the security risk of carrying large amounts of cash. BNPL companies work on the exact same basis. They take a cut of the sale and pocket it. Then they collect the money from you over three payments.

So what's the problem? I think if we can get over the first problem — the fact that one in three people don't even realise they are taking out a loan — and we can live in hope that the experience of payday loans won't be repeated with BNPL, we can start to identify some of the other problems.

A bit like PCP (which we'll cover in the next section), one of the things BNPL encourages people to do is to buy stuff they would not have bought at all; and when they do buy, one BNPL provider suggests that the amount of money they spend increases by 40%. People have openly admitted they would not have bought at all if BNPL wasn't available. So even if you were always planning on buying X, you actually increase your spend by €40 for every €100 you were planning on spending – just because you can pay it over three interest-free repayments. Even if it did end up at 0%, if you were originally going to spend €100 and spent €140 instead, that smells like €40 in 'interest' to me. Dress it up however you want, it's €40 more out of your pocket than you had planned.

We also have to look at the fact that people who use these services often have more than one loan outstanding at any given time. They are so easy to get into and therefore you can very quickly find yourself with lots of different payments coming out at different times of the month with no real idea in your head when each of them started, what they are for or when they are due to finish. This can give rise to confusion, result in late or missed payment charges and also, which surprises lots of people, affect your credit rating, as missed payments can be recorded on your credit report.

I have a genuine fear about BNPL. I wish I didn't; in fact I have never wanted more to be wrong about a financial product. But I just feel BNPL is far too accessible, it is incredibly user-friendly, it is absolutely everywhere and it is obvious the vast majority of people do not know what they are signing up to.

If you can't afford it today, I'm sorry, but you can't afford it.

The reality is you are reading this book because you want to reach financial independence at the earliest possible point in your life and you want to do it without sacrificing your enjoyment of today. Borrowing often gives you an immediate boost of happiness or joy because you get that new car or you buy those new shoes or you go on that lovely holiday. But it is a financial treadmill and it is very hard to move forward when you are going backwards. Spending the money you draw down from a loan can often feel good but, remember, that means you have to tackle your finances with a financial hangover.

I cannot stress this enough. Clearing your expensive debt

is right up there as one of the most important financial tasks you have on your road to financial independence. Ignore it and you are destined to a financial life of back and forth and will probably end up achieving a lot less than you would have without the debt.

3. Thinking a new car is a requirement

We also need to be conscious of the changes borrowing makes to how much we spend. A perfect example of this is car loans. If you are using savings to buy a car you are much more cost sensitive than you are when borrowing to buy. For example, let's say you have €50,000 in savings to buy a car. You spot one you are really happy with for €40,000 and there is another with a few extras for €45,000. The difference is €5,000 and it is very easy to quantify that difference in your head. You then make an informed decision as to whether the difference is worth it for you. If you are borrowing for the car, €40,000 over five years will cost you roughly €811 per month. But €45,000 over the same period is only an extra €101 per month, or, as a good car salesperson might say to you, 'That's less than €25 per week for the car you really want, sure that's only one Chinese takeaway a week. Now do you want the car you really want or a Chinese meal?'

This trick has been around a long time. Not only does it bring the amount in your head from almost €1,000 per month down to €25 a week, it also asks you to compare a Chinese takeaway (which, some might argue, isn't good for you anyway) with a shiny new car with all the extras that is going to make you feel good.

This example of how we can be manoeuvred or even manipulated into spending more on a car is just the tip of the iceberg. When it comes to PCP this is where it comes into its own. For those lucky enough not to know what PCP is, at its very basic level; it is where you rent a car under the guise that you think you actually own it. You go to a dealer and buy, typically, a brand-new car. You make a down payment in the form of cash or a trade-in and then you guess what mileage you are going to do in the car over the term of the agreement, which is often three years. The garage then calculates the minimum amount of money the car will be worth in three years if you stick to the mileage and keep the car in good condition. The clever bit here, from a salesperson's point of view, is that they only finance the bit in the middle, dramatically reducing the repayments.

So, for example, you see a car for €50,000, you put down a deposit/trade-in of €10,000 and they work out that in three years' time, if you do no more than the mileage you've agreed, the car will be worth €10,000. Now all they have to do is provide finance for the €30,000 in the middle.

In very basic terms, you go from having to cover the cost of a €40,000 loan to only having to service a €30,000 loan. Guess what happens? You end up buying a car that has a much higher sticker price than you would have originally chosen because you find the monthly repayments manageable and your brain decides to turn off the fact that in three years' time, if you want

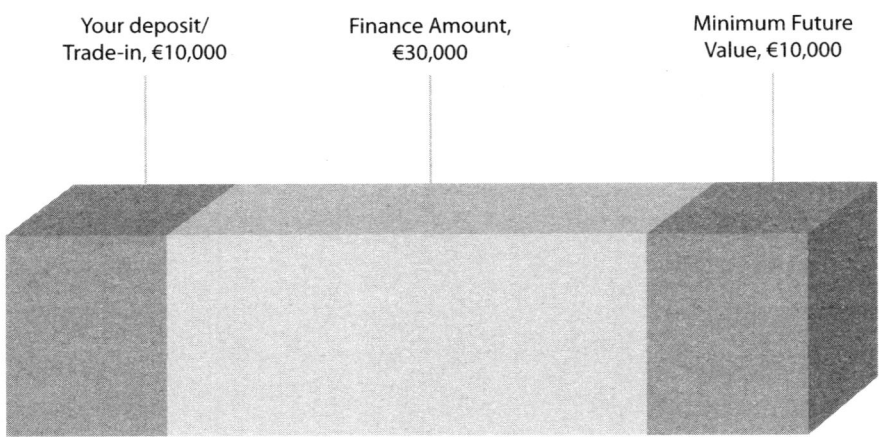

Your deposit/Trade-in, €10,000   Finance Amount, €30,000   Minimum Future Value, €10,000

to actually own the car, you have to come up with €10,000. Most people don't come up with the €10,000; instead they roll into a new PCP agreement and the cycle repeats itself.

My guilty pleasure is cars. I love a nice car. As I get older I feel I am getting a bit wiser, but I am not perfect. I had been driving the same car for about four or five years and earlier this year I convinced myself several times that I needed to change. I fought the urge a few times. I did this with some tricks I have picked up over the years. The easiest and most effective trick, I find, is a good valet. If you keep looking for reasons why you *need* to change your car, get it a good deep clean – not just a car wash, a proper job. I find this buys me months before the urges start to crop up again. In fact I would suggest this trick alone had me in that car for an extra 12 months in total.

Remember, car dealers are there to make money, and they make money when you change your car. You are paying for the privilege, so the longer you delay changing your car and the less often you do it, the more money you save. When you get to the point where you have to change your car because it's unreliable, dangerous, too heavy on fuel etc., remind yourself of this: you are going to get rid of your car and unless it's actually at the end of its shelf life somebody else is going to buy it and they are going to be delighted with it. Think about that for a minute – you have convinced yourself you must get rid of it, yet somebody else will be delighted to get it and in the middle is the car dealer making money off you both.

Anyway, as I said, cars are my guilty pleasure. So I started playing with the app in the evenings looking at cars. Now one rule I always stick to when buying cars is that I will never buy a car under two years old. The way I see it is that you lose a fortune on a new car the minute you drive it off the forecourt. Some figures suggest that in the first two years you lose somewhere between 30% and 60% of the value of a car. Of course there will always be anomalies, but those figures are stark. Imagine that for every €10,000 you spend on a new car, two years later you will have lost between €3,000 and €6,000. That's why I always buy cars that are at least two years old. Let someone else take that hit and I will pick up where they left off.

So I started looking at two-year-old cars. Then one of those anomalies cropped up: whatever was happening in the second-hand market for the type of car I was looking at there was very little difference between the cost of a two-year-old model and the cost of a one-year-old version. On paper, it was now looking like for a small amount extra it made much more sense to buy a one-year-old car. Once the garage had me focused on the one-year-old price it struck again with the 'Eoin, do you know for not much more you can have a brand-new one, in the colour you want? And if you're financing it I can offer 4.9% on the new car but I can only give you 7.9% on the one-year-old car.'

Then came the next sales pitch: 'And if you are planning on financing it then the repayments on the PCP on this new car are actually 40% lower per month than an ordinary hire purchase agreement.'

I'll be honest, I was taken in. For the first time in my life I was considering buying a brand-new car. The figures for the two-year-old car just made no sense. I was going to buy and I was even considering not using my own cash. Then my own words hit me: the 72-hour rule …

> The 72-hour rule is one of the most popular rules I have ever come out with. The idea is that every time you want to buy something, put it back. If you still want to buy it 72 hours later it is probably something you should actually buy or something that will actually add value to your life. You see, 72 hours is just enough time to decide if you want or even need this thing or if it's something you are buying on a whim or because some marketing department got into your head to tell you that you should buy it. One of three things happens when you apply the 72-hour rule:

HOW TO ACHIEVE FINANCIAL FREEDOM | 63

> 1. After, let's say, 24 hours you find something else, not necessarily cheaper but better, and you start the 72 hours on that.
> 2. After 96 hours or so you remember you forgot to buy it and accept that it was never for you.
> 3. You buy it after 72 hours.
>
> A couple of things to bear in mind when applying the rule. You can't set an alarm on your phone – if you forget, then it just wasn't meant to be, that's the point of the rule. Also, you don't apply the 72-hour rule to purchases like bread and milk!
>
> You might ask, 'What if the thing I want is gone when I go back after 72 hours?' Well, that, my friend, is destiny. Forget it and move on with your life.

So I applied my 72-hour rule and guess what happened. About 24 hours later something occurred to me. The difference between the price of a two-year-old car and a brand-new one is very little. But I thought to myself 'I wonder how much a 3 year old one is.' When I checked I was shocked to find that the three-year-old car was 40% cheaper than the new one. It was an anomaly! I ended up buying a three-year-old car. Driving along the M50 in it about 20 minutes after I collected it I remember thinking, as any good financial planner would, I love this car more than I would have if I had bought a new one. You see once I drove it off the forecourt it was second-hand, but it still smelled new, it was spotlessly clean and it had very few signs of wear and tear. It felt good and I was happy, but for me professionally it was a lucky escape!

Cars are an interesting social phenomenon. For many people they make a statement. For others they mean nothing. I have spent years justifying my car purchasing habits by telling myself I need a good reliable car or because I deal with people's money I need to present the right image. As I've got older, or maybe just wiser, this is wearing thin, but I never really understood how far I had come until recently. It was just before I had changed my car and unusually for me I was meeting a client outside the office, and when the meeting was over he walked me to my car in the car park. At the time I was driving a six-year-old Audi, a nice car that looked well. I had been looking at other cars earlier that day and I mentioned I was thinking of changing my car, to which my client replied, 'Yeah, I would have expected you to be driving something better than this.'

Younger me would have been mortified. I would have driven away thinking, does the client not think I am successful? Have they lost confidence in me now? But I didn't feel like that. I actually felt confident in the reply I gave, which was 'I've reached the point in my life where I choose to spend my money on other things. Cars are important to me, I love them, but there are more important things.'

The client didn't disagree, in fact I think it showed that I lived by what I was trying to get him to do with his money. The next time I met him I was driving a new car – to me, the three-year-old-one I had bought. Now wouldn't I have looked stupid in a brand-new one?

Car loans really can put us on the back foot, particularly when it comes to trying to keep up with the Joneses. Remember, when you see a friend or neighbour driving a new car, don't think 'Wow, nice new car', think 'Wow, nice new loan' because chances are that's what it is, a new loan, and the cycle continues.

4. Not regularly checking your accounts/spending

When I meet a new client for the first time I ask them to complete a form. Part of the form asks the individual or couple to fill in how much they spend. It lists everything from holidays to fuel, groceries, utility bills, eating out, clothes … I think you get the point.

What I find really interesting is just how often people declare with absolute shock, 'I had no idea we were spending so much on X!' Sometimes the shock is just about how much they spend in general. These people are intelligent, clued-in people. The shock isn't because they aren't aware of their day-to-day spending, it's more that they don't see the wood for the trees. They go about their daily lives, they see money going out of the account, but they never actually take a step back and look at the bigger picture. It's like an aeroplane that takes off from Los Angeles, heading to New York, but its nose is just one degree off. When it lands, it is actually 80 km off track. The point is that nobody notices the one degree but everyone recognises they are in New Jersey and not New York when they get there.

For lots of reasons we should be checking our accounts regularly, including checking for fraud or errors.

5. Not having your money working as hard as you do

We all work hard – you might argue you work harder than other people, and you might be right. But when it comes to creating real wealth there is absolutely no point in working hard and making good money and then having your money sitting around lazily enjoying life in a bank account.

If you have €10,000 sitting in a bank account today and you leave it there for five years, ignoring tax and assuming 0.5% deposit interest, that €10,000 is going to turn into €10,250.

If you want to buy something today for €10,000 and you decide to wait until your bank account matures in five years' time, assuming 2% inflation, again using simple interest, the thing that costs €10,000 today will cost €11,000 in five years' time.

Most people look at their bank account and think 'Oh wow, it went from €10,000 to €10,250 – I made €250', but when you look at the thing you wanted to buy you actually lost €750 of what is called your purchasing power.

This is a perfect example of your money not working hard for you.

Think about it in a different light. Imagine you're on a salary of €50,000 and it costs you exactly €50,000 to live your life (for simplicity I am ignoring tax again). Over the next 20 years, in an ordinary functioning economic world, your cost of living, allowing for inflation of 2%, is going to go from €50,000 to €74,297. So if your pay doesn't increase at least in line with that over that period, you are actually going backwards.

Most people work for somebody else and can't control how much they will earn next year. But whether that's the case for you or you are your own boss, you need to control the things you can control, and one of the things that is in your control is how you use and invest your money. You are much better served expending your energy on the things you can control instead of wasting energy on things you can't. How hard your money works is totally within your control.

Why aren't you doing it? People often say, 'I don't know how' or 'Investing is risky' or the straightforward 'I am scared to.' These are all excuses, but they are not reasons and later in the book I will help you with some of those excuses.

6. Deciding you are not good with money

If you tell yourself you are crap with money, guess what? You're right. But if you tell yourself you are good with money, guess what? You're right. We've touched on this already in this book so I won't labour the point, but our brain is there to serve us. At its core it is a fight-or-flight decision-making mechanism. It is there to give us the information we need to decide if we are right or if we should change our decisions. But unfortunately our brain is not completely independent.

Every office or workplace has a 'Yes person'. Let's call them Sam. The boss in your office loves Sam because Sam always agrees with them. Sam feeds off this attention, he loves it. So he constantly seeks ways of getting more of this attention. Sam does this by listening to what the boss says and then going off and finding information to present to the boss to show the boss they are right.

Your brain is your Sam and you are the boss. You brain constantly looks for information in the world to confirm you are on the right track but, ironically, your brain does not have an independent thought. Your brain only acts on the instructions you give it, so if you tell Sam you are crap with money Sam will say 'Yes, you are' and then constantly provide you with information in a never-ending feedback loop to confirm you are correct.

You can stop the feedback loop by changing the narrative. Simply tell Sam you are great with money and then Sam will find things in the world to confirm that you are right. Don't get me wrong, the mistakes we all make with our money don't disappear because we have a chat with Sam – they still exist. It is just that Sam focuses on them less and seeks out the things you are doing that confirm you are good with money.

So you arrive home from a day clothes shopping and old Sam

would be reminding you about how much you spent, but new, positive Sam will be all about how much you saved because you waited for the sales instead of going out last week when everything was 20% more expensive. (I'm deliberately ignoring whether you needed to go shopping at all!)

I am not saying that speaking to your Sam positively is definitely going to change your world, but it just might. One thing I can give you a cast-iron guarantee of is that speaking to Sam positively will do a lot more good than the amount you will be dragged back by speaking negatively to Sam.

7. Not educating yourself

'I am not good with money, so what's the point?' is something I hear time and time again from people who have just written themselves off financially and decided they are not even going to try to change the way things are, just 'because'.

It reminds me of a conversation I had with a personal trainer. We were going through what I do and don't eat and I said, 'I don't like vegetables.' He looked at me and said, 'You're an adult – grow up', and he was right. Deciding I didn't like an entire food group was just ridiculous and childish and he was right to call me out on it.

So you need to call yourself out on this too if you're in a similar position. The likelihood is that you are not in this position because you are reading this book, which means you are open to learning. But I promise you have someone in your life who has this attitude and they need to be told to 'eat their vegetables'. You need to be the one to call them out on it. Unless they are eight years old. There is no excuse in the world we live in and the information available to us all not to educate yourself on money. After all, money is an integral part of our lives and not understanding it will set you up for a life full of challenges.

8. Not being honest

People do it; they don't get all the facts so they can be in ignorant bliss about their money. By not doing the work and getting the facts, people convince themselves the problem isn't as bad as it could be, or – worse – they think ignoring the problem somehow magically makes it go away.

When we were filming *How to be Good with Money* I saw it time and time again. Some of the contributors came on the show to force themselves to face their reality because they could not muster either the strength or the courage to do it for themselves. There was a section in the show where I had done an analysis on their finances and I sat down with them to talk them through it. This was very entertaining for the viewer but many of the contributors would say both on and off camera that they were terrified about what I was about to tell them. They never had truly faced their finances and here they were in an office surrounded by an entire crew, camera in their face and a nation watching from home and they were about to be confronted with their truth. My dentist later described to me that he used to watch the people on the show walk into my office and he said he imagined it was how certain people felt coming to see him for an extraction.

The fear for the people going to the dentist was as real as it was for some people facing their finances.

9. Thinking the big moves are more impactful than the small ones

I struggle with my weight. As I write I am carrying much more weight than I was a few years ago and definitely more than I am happy to. And it gets me down. Then, when it gets me down, I spiral into making the wrong choices and gaining more weight. A few years ago I lost a huge amount of weight and I felt good about myself, but even then I didn't feel I had reached where I wanted to be. In other words, I couldn't recognise how much is enough, which interestingly is a key objective when doing a financial plan, working out how much is enough. But I always wanted a little bit more, just tone this, or lose those few pounds. I was happier with how I felt then, but I still wasn't fully satisfied.

Looking back on that time now I would love to be any weight between where I am right now and where I was then. I tell myself that I would appreciate it this time.

The interesting thing is that when I was losing weight I didn't notice as each day went by that things were getting better, that I was actually losing weight. We make small decisions each day that seem to make no difference when we wake up in the morning. Then one day you pull on a T-shirt and it just feels a little looser, or somebody says you look great or asks, 'Have you lost weight?' (Whether they should or shouldn't ask that question is outside the scope of this book!)

When I started to notice these things, as I started to change shape, when my runs started getting easier and I could go faster with what felt like less effort, it all helped me move forward. You think to yourself, 'Why would I make the silly little mistakes when I'm making all this progress? What's the point of getting up early to go for a run if I'm going to sabotage that later in the day with some silly decision?'

But when I was getting in shape the last time I actually allowed myself the big mistakes. So, for example, I might enjoy a big night out, or I'd go out for a lavish meal and even have dessert. I recognised this was part of me and it was a part of me I didn't want to give up. But provided I was doing the small things right most of the time, making 'big mistakes' less frequently actually had less impact on my progress than you might imagine. Where it all falls apart, for me anyway, is when I am not doing the small things right. Then I think to myself, 'What difference does it make if I do the big things wrong? Sure the entire thing is a mess.'

The lessons we learn from looking after ourselves and our weight are very valuable when you transfer them to our finances. It is probably why hearing 'fitfluencers' online talking about getting in shape resonates with me, not just because I need to get in shape but because there are so many similarities between the things they say and what way we should be handling our money. Doing the small things right repeatedly will have much more positive impact on our long-term financial future and achieving financial independence than some of the things we think are either big wins or big mistakes.

There were two guys in an office I used to work in. They both worked in sales. But they each took a very different approach. To protect them both and to avoid getting that 'Why did you tell everyone about me?' complaint the next time I run into them, let's call them Salt and Pepper.

Pepper was very consistent with their sales, always picking up the smaller sales, and would never have a week with a blank sheet. They put the graft in, worked hard and were very consistent. Every sale was equally important, no matter how small it was.

Salt, on the other hand, had a very different approach. They were always chasing the 'big' sale. They loved the chase, they put lots of groundwork in to get the big juicy ones over the line. Their sales were very infrequent but when the odd one landed there was lots of talk around the office – 'Did you hear about the big sale Salt got?' Salt always felt good about landing these sales and it drove them on to chase more down.

The interesting thing is that over time Pepper's overall figures were better, in fact much better, because one of the things that was happening was Pepper was consistently doing the small stuff and then from time to time landing a big sale. When the big sale came it was a 'bonus' and Pepper's figures were boosted. Whereas with Salt when the big sale came in it would only just make up for all the blank weeks and get back on target.

It is classic tortoise and hare stuff, except with the added benefit that every so often our tortoise (Pepper) had a sprint (a big sale).

The exact same thing happens with your personal finance. When you concentrate on getting the little things right it helps you focus on making the right decision when it comes to the big stuff. But also, as with my weight loss journey, when you put the work into the small stuff it gives you the encouragement to not sabotage it all with a silly big decision. Nowhere is this more evident than with money that doing the little things right works every time; it's just that sometimes we need to look at things a little differently.

Little things done right repeatedly result in big things happening over time. When we get caught in chasing only the big things or we get bogged down because something goes wrong, even drastically wrong, we often lose sight of the bigger picture and sometimes we even destroy the progress we have made.

Things are going to go wrong but they have a lot less impact when we are doing the little things right.

10. Having a little bit of knowledge

We all have that one friend who is an expert in every single topic that comes up. They have strong opinions and they deliver those opinions with such confidence that it is hard to question them. Sometimes they even convince us we are wrong about something only for us later to discover we should have stuck to our guns.

Often when you scratch the surface with these people you find their knowledge to be superficial and they are the jack of all trades and master of none. After a while you get accustomed to these people and you stop taking advice or forming opinions from listening to them.

But what if that person is you? Would you recognise it in yourself? The problem here is that we may not be presenting these traits in all aspects of our life but, for some reason, when it comes to money we can all be an expert. This overconfidence isn't an issue if you have an opinion on how long it will take you to complete a marathon, or if you're predicting who will win the All-Ireland. But when it comes to our money it can have impact and unfortunately it can do damage.

I have had experience with these people in private practice. They are very measured throughout the entire financial planning process and then when it comes to discussing how to invest their money, which we do in a simple, slow, boring way, all of a sudden they are full of opinions about how all the knowledge I have gathered in the last 25+ years is wrong, how my education and experience is incorrect and how they know the way to do it right.

I get it, I understand where they are coming from. It's just money, after all. You use it to buy things and you try your best to store it up so you have some left over to use later. Simple, right? But it is also part of everyday life. We interact with it and think about money multiple times every day and that breathes a familiarity into us that can lead us to become overly confident. This familiarity can lead to opinions, and although

I fully encourage people developing their own opinions about money, there is a difference between having your own opinions and having your own facts.

I'm treading a very fine line here, because I genuinely do want people to form opinions, I want people to think about their money, I want to encourage us all to challenge the status quo and how things are done. But sometimes it does become frustrating. I listen intently to a point and provide factual data that refutes the opinion and the data is ignored or dismissed. When I ask where the information that formed their opinion came from they don't see any issue that their mate Kev, who is a bricklayer, did it and it worked for him, so it must be good.

I am being extreme here, but the opinions and biases we carry can often be a lot more subtle than how I have described them. You need to be aware of your own and you need to question their source. I am not saying you need to put them to one side, but you do need to validate them, ideally with facts, not your mate Kev's opinion.

11. Getting advice from the wrong place

It doesn't matter what area of life we are talking about, a little bit of knowledge can be a dangerous thing, and for me this is never more true than when we talk about money. We are a country that in general doesn't talk about money. We are often better at listening to stories about other people's money woes, trials and tribulations. Let's be fair, though; we could do with a little work on getting a similar satisfaction hearing about people's successes.

So we like to know about money but we don't like to talk openly about our own. My Q&A on a Saturday on Instagram is a perfect example. Every Saturday I put up a question box, and the questions roll in. A typical Saturday will see somewhere between 800 and 1,200 questions hit my Insta inbox. Here's the interesting bit: when I reply, everyone sees the question and everyone sees my answer, but nobody gets to see who asked the question, so the asker's anonymity is protected. It's perfect for a country that likes to talk about other people's money but not their own.

The problem with this societal norm is that if we don't engage in open conversations about money we are less likely to discuss new information we come across with our peers and more likely to accept things on face value because we don't have a proper sounding board. Nobody likes to feel silly when they're asking a question. Add money into the mix and it's a perfect melting pot for misinformation being dispensed by people who are unqualified to give it. I see these situations all the time. People get a little nugget of information online about some financial trick or hack, assume it's gospel and then try to implement it in their own lives.

When we are in a position that we don't learn much from each other about our finances but we want to learn, it can lead us down the path of finding out things for ourselves. Traditionally this wasn't a bad thing because it meant you went to a bookshop or library and bought or borrowed a book by a respected author, usually an expert in their field, who had an editor and publishing team in the background to fact check and crosscheck everything. Today you can be watching an episode of *Fair City* with your phone in your hand getting day-trading tips from somebody who last week was famous for spice bag reviews.

These tips and tricks, whether they're on day trading or crypto or how to budget properly, are often well intended but sometimes they are an out-and-out scam. But either way, when they go wrong they can be incredibly costly, both financially and emotionally.

You see, implementing bad advice can be costly. That cost can often be measured as a monetary amount. But it's harder to quantify the emotional damage people suffer when things do go wrong. I have met countless numbers of people who 'don't like investing' because either they or somebody close to them lost money on bank shares, and I still to this day meet people who were emotionally impacted by their experience with Eircom shares. These people have had an experience that has scarred them financially for life and resulted in them being held back because they cannot find a way to get over it mentally. I find I can talk some people down and get them back on the straight and narrow, but these are often people that are more open to listening – they came into my office, after all. It's the people who just point blank refuse to open the door at all who worry me the most.

The world has moved fast in recent years and we are in the privileged position of having information on any topic we want at our fingertips. But there is a difference between information and education. Educating yourself on a topic requires a commitment. It is a commitment worth investing in but you need to be careful along the way. When you get burned once it can have lasting financial and emotional impact. The one true way to ensure you avoid some of these mistakes is to choose your sources and guidance well and, most important of all, be happy to follow the mantra 'I am very happy to get rich slow.'

12. Not writing stuff down

I am sure there is science somewhere to back this up, but I believe that taking out a pen and paper and writing stuff down has more impact than just typing it into our phones or laptops. It just goes deeper into our brains.

One really clever thing I have seen work time and time again is to use the pen and paper for three things:

1. Financial goals
2. Spending habits
3. Your one-page financial plan.

Let's look at each in turn.

First, our financial goals. It just makes sense that if what we write on paper goes a little deeper, writing down where we want to get to financially is going to have an impact too. It gives us something to strive towards but also acts as a reminder of what we are trying to achieve and may make some of the sacrifices along the way more palatable. But it also offers something else. When we look back in the future at our written financial goals it is often a reminder of how things change. You see, something that is important for us to achieve today may become irrelevant to the future us because our priorities might have changed. Seeing this happen repeatedly is valuable in itself, but it also acts as a reminder that when things go wrong and we are forced to change, that's okay. Sometimes, even when things don't go wrong, we change our priorities anyway.

Second, writing down your spending habits is something I have been suggesting for years. I suggest that for a week, don't change your spending habits but every time you spend money take out your phone, go into the notes section and record what you spent money on and how much you spent, for example 'coffee €3.50'. At the end of the week take out a pen and paper, draw a line down the middle of the page and write Conscious Spending at the top of one column and Subconscious Spending at the top of the other. Or you can use the alternative and equally powerful headings Added Value to My Life and Didn't Add Value to My Life. Now take out the notes sections of your phone and categorise everything you spent money on in the last week. This is a great way to track what you are spending on that is adding value to your life and, more important, will help you strip out the stuff that isn't. Doing this a few times a year really prevents things like Parkinson's law and wallet leakage (which we'll discuss later) creeping in.

The third thing you should be writing down is your financial plan. Take out a sheet of paper and divide it into four quadrants. Write the headings Own, Owe, Earn and Spend and then go about filling in the blanks. We will cover this more fully a little later, but this is a powerful exercise that becomes more powerful when you do it year after year and when you look back to see how things have changed.

13. Leaving the back door open

I have seen it again and again: people are on the pig's back, accumulating savings, building wealth and funding their pension, and the future looks bright. Until it doesn't. They get sick and everything gets derailed, they have to dip into their savings to keep bread and milk on the table, the mortgage repayments go on pause and the pension contributions just have to wait. Obviously an illness is a huge setback physically, but it can also set them back years financially. It is bad when people get sick; it is worse again for families if somebody dies.

Illness isn't avoidable, but the financial fallout certainly is. Building a financial plan but not having the right life cover, specified illness cover and income protection in place is like having an amazing home full of lovely valuable things and then going out and leaving the back door open; it might be fine, but if somebody does get in it will be costly.

I have seen both sides of this, I have seen people suffer a financial crisis in the middle of a medical one and then I have seen people who have cover in place. It would be a stretch for me to say that in the middle of it all these people getting payouts are delighted they got sick and I have never seen anybody happy somebody died because of the life cover payout but at a time in people's lives that is full of uncertainty, having the right insurance payout come in and knowing you can concentrate on the medical problems or, worse, a loss and not worry about money is invaluable.

14. Paying too much tax

Let's do a little quiz:

Question 1: Would you prefer to:
A Pay less tax than you need to?
B Pay more tax than you need to?

Question 2: Would you prefer to save with:
A Your income before the taxman takes any money out of it?
B Your after-tax income, i.e. after the taxman has taken their cut?

Question 3: Would you prefer:
A Your savings to grow tax free?
B To pay tax on the growth of your savings?

Obviously the answer to these three questions is A. Of course you want to pay less tax, save from your before-tax income, not your after-tax income; and you want to avoid paying tax on your growth. This is available to every worker in the country and is the envy of many other jurisdictions. It is our pension system.

Yet so many people simply say, 'I don't like pensions' or 'My friend lost all their pension so I wouldn't touch one.' But a pension is simply a savings plan that has very heavy tax incentives, such as tax relief on the way in, tax-free growth and a tax-free lump sum at retirement.

Yes, you do have to pay income tax on some of the money, but the maths still works out in your favour. There is no more tax-efficient way for a PAYE worker to save for their future selves than using a pension.

Staying away from them because your friends had a bad experience with them is like saying 'I don't like food because my friend got food poisoning.' We have one of the best pensions systems in the world. There have been awful investments that people have put their pensions into, but that's the fault of poor investment advice, not the pensions themselves.

When it comes to company owners and some very senior executives who are shareholders, pensions are just as attractive, but if you fall into that category you do have some other things to consider, such as retirement relief and maybe even entrepreneurial relief, but still for most of your career your pension should be the main focus as the tool of choice for extracting wealth from the business in a tax-efficient manner.

If you have a pension, well done, but that doesn't mean you aren't still making mistakes. Too often I come across people who are putting in, let's say, 3% of their salary and getting a 3% match from their employer. However, if they went up to 5% their employer would also go to 5%.

Also remember that you personally can pay between 15%

and 40% of your salary into a pension, depending on your age. People often don't realise they can put more in than what is coming out from the 'main scheme'.

If you aren't putting in the maximum required to get the maximum match from your employer and assuming you can afford it if you aren't using up your full personal allowance, you are basically telling your boss you don't want that pay rise and you are telling the taxman you are happy to pay more tax than you need to.

15. Making emotional decisions instead of financial ones

Sometimes the heart drives the head, and that's okay, but sometimes not doing something because of some emotional reason is a mistake. Somebody approached me on the street recently with a query about specified illness cover, but as the conversation developed something else came to my attention that highlights how our emotions can cloud our judgement. I discovered that they had a little over €21,000 sitting in a bank deposit account but they were also carrying €2,000 on a credit card.

When I asked why they didn't just clear the credit card and, ideally, cut it up, they looked not just horrified at the thought but also gave me one of those looks – the kind that usually only a sibling can deliver – that screamed 'Are you stupid?'

So I pushed a little further and I explained that the interest on the credit card in simple interest terms was €400 per year, that it was silly to be paying that when they weren't getting interest at that level from the bank on the money they had on deposit – in fact, in simple interest terms they were, at best, getting about €200 per year on their full €21,000.

It still didn't seem to be landing, so I went on: 'So basically you have given the bank €21,000 and they pay you €200 interest for that. The bank then takes €2,000 of your own money and lends it back to you on the credit card they sold you and they charge you €400 in interest. The bank are giving you back your own money.' (Before anyone goes off to get me cancelled for my simplified maths, remember that this was a person who had stopped me on the street – I was trying to make it understandable!)

Although my point had landed it was what they said next that made the penny drop. 'But I can't touch my savings, it's my savings.' In other words, they had an emotional attachment to the savings, it probably gave them a financial security blanket, and wrapped in each and every one of those €21,000 was 21,000 sacrifices that had been made to build that pot. This person could not see the error of their ways and although I think they understood my rationale, and although it made perfect sense to them that what they were doing was wrong, I still think it's 50:50 whether they actually went and cleared the credit card after our chat. Unfortunately I'll never know.

There are times when emotion does trump finance. For example, clearing the mortgage. This is a calculation I get asked to run several times a week for different clients. They have enough savings to clear their mortgage in full and they want to know if it makes financial sense. The reality is that in the vast majority of cases there are better things to do with your money that will result in a better financial outcome. I did one of these calculations recently: the client had just drawn down a whopper of a mortgage of just under €1,000,000 over 30 years and they were totally comfortable making the repayments. They also had some money coming to them in the next 12 months or so and they wanted to know if they should clear their mortgage when it came in. Now, before we go through the maths I recognise that most people don't have a €1,000,000 mortgage, but the maths is the same.

When I ran the numbers I found that this person was going to end up paying back just under €1,850,000 in total repayments. In other words, their cost of credit, the amount of interest they were going to pay, was €850,000 (obviously I am rounding the numbers). Now if they cleared the mortgage they would save €850,000 in interest. That sounds like the best option, right? Who doesn't want to save €850,000 in interest? But if they took the €1 million and invested it they would need to get a net tax return of 2.07% per annum over 30 years on an investment for it to make sense to invest the money instead of clearing the mortgage. To put that into perspective, the portfolio we use for medium-risk investors has given a gross return of 7.05% per annum over the last 20 years, so 2.07% net is far from a wild forecast of growth.

However, there is huge emotional benefit to clearing your mortgage. Even when the maths is this stark, if I thought the client would sleep better at night if the mortgage were gone I would give them the facts to make an informed decision and if they decided to use their money to help them sleep at night I certainly wouldn't stand in their way.

Mixing emotion with finance can really muddy the waters. Sometimes it is useful, sometimes it isn't. Your trick to use it to your advantage is to ask yourself, when making a financial decision, is this decision based on fact or based on my feelings?

16. Allowing lifestyle creep to kick in

When was the last time you got a pay rise? Can you think back to before you got the pay rise? Maybe things were a little tight and you thought, 'If I can just get this pay rise it will allow me to get ahead.' How are things now? Still tight? Do you think you need another bump in salary to try to get ahead of things?

There are two things at play here. One is that we have just come through one of the highest levels of inflation we have seen in years. The cost of everything has dramatically increased and if your pay hasn't increased with it you will have gone backwards.

> People often think the best way to beat inflation is through a pay rise, but it's not that simple. Let's imagine inflation is at 10%. If you get a 10% pay rise, well done, you have beaten inflation. But if everyone in the country gets a 10% pay rise all it does is increase demand, and supply won't have caught up, resulting in inflation pushing up even further. Inflation at its simplest is the cost of stuff

today compared to the cost of the same stuff this time last year. If, for example, a basket of goods cost €100 this day last year and the same basket of goods costs €110 today, that's 10% inflation. At its core, inflation is driven by supply and demand. For example if I have ten widgets to sell and only five people want to buy them, it means supply is high and demand is low, so I will probably have to bring my price down. But if a hundred people want to buy my ten widgets, supply is low and demand is high so, as the seller, I will get away with increasing my price.

Going back to our pay rise, if things go up in price by 10% fewer people can afford them so demand goes down, but if everyone gets a 10% pay rise, demand goes up again and the factors that originally drove prices up in the first place, if they are not resolved, kick in again and the rising prices continue and the spiral of upward prices continues.

Lifestyle creep occurs even when we aren't going through or are just out of a period of high inflation. It's all to do with Parkinson's law. Parkinson's law is the rule that says a task will take as long as you give it. So if you have an hour to cut the grass it will take an hour, but if you have three hours to cut the grass it will take three hours. The same applies to your money. If you make €50,000 a year you spend €50,000; if you earn €60,000 you spend €60,000 because lifestyle creep kicks in and your lifestyle expands to fill the income you have. Hence, when I ask somebody how life has changed since their last pay rise they usually say it's exactly the same at it was.

The easiest way to combat lifestyle creep is to work out exactly what you need on a month-to-month basis, not to live a tight life, but to live a comfortable life that you are happy with. Once you have done this you need to work out your total take-home pay each month and hopefully you identify a surplus of income above expenditure. To reverse lifestyle creep you need to be very intentional with what happens to that surplus. You need to allocate it to savings, or clear off debt or put it in your pension. If you aren't intentional, lifestyle creep kicks in and you spend it just because it is there.

Remember, allocating this money with intent should not result in the joy being sucked out of your life because when you worked out your expenses you allowed for a comfortable life.

17. Wallet leakage

Wallet leakage and lifestyle creep often hang around together, but there is a difference. Wallet leakage is where you find your money is just vanishing and you really aren't sure where to. This is the subscription you signed up to that you haven't used in months or the utility bill that you have just left with the same provider for years despite the fact that you have long ago been taken off the new customer rate and are now paying an exorbitant existing customer rate.

Leakage is the small repetitive stuff that goes unnoticed, often for long periods of time, but it is also the type of stuff we add to without thinking. For example, there was a time when none of us had any streaming services, but now it's not unusual to find people with Netflix, Disney+, Amazon Prime etc. We make these decisions to sign up in an isolated bubble without really cross-referencing other similar products we already have; we just think 'Sure it's only €8.99 per month. I'd pay that to see this film in the cinema and now I can see the film and have an entire month of other content for a similar price.'

These companies thrive on this. Take Spotify, for example. They have built a very successful business on making it easy to sign up, they have become very good at encouraging you to step up from free to premium by making free accessible in the first place to draw you in but for it also to be just annoying enough that the cost of premium feels less painful than the annoyance of the ads. But one of the key factors in their success is their retention rate. Research suggests that 77% of customers who sign up to Spotify keep it. But it is the level they go to and the detail they capture to improve their 'retention rates' that fascinate me. We are just going about our lives using their service, half oblivious to the fact that every time we use their service they are garnishing details about our behaviour to work out how to keep us and how to learn from us to keep other customers. Their retention rate is up 3% compared to 2024 figures, and when you already keep three out of every four customers you have, finding an extra 3% is admirable. They analyse everything; for example, they know paying customers are more likely to stay (84% retention) than free customers, so they push us to become paying customers asap. But they also know that people who listen to podcasts are more likely to hang around; overall, podcast listeners have a 19% higher retention rate than music-only listeners. But those who create playlists have a whopping 34% higher retention rate than those who don't. I admire Spotify for what they do and how they do it, and if they recognise that creating playlists is a key retention factor and therefore make creating playlists easier and a better user experience for me, the customer, we both win. What I am trying to flag here is the fact that all this stuff, all this analysis is going on in the background and in the meantime we don't really recognise it and we just think we are making a conscious decision each month for that bit of money to leave our bank account and go to theirs.

It is easy to explain wallet leakage by focusing on just subscriptions, but it goes further than that; it is basically any spend that occurs regularly and that we don't really give any conscious thought to. It is small things like the utility bill, but it is also big things like the mortgage. You could argue that buying your sixth coffee of the day because you walked by your favourite barista and sure you always buy a coffee when you walk by them, is also wallet leakage. Wallet leakage is the recurring automatic spending of money, whether that automation is by direct debit or by habit.

My suggestion here is that you sit down and review all your regular spending for wallet leakage. Again, let's focus on subscriptions, which are easy to understand, but you go through a similar process with all your leakage. Ask yourself one simple question: 'If I were a new customer looking at this service for the first time would I buy it?' If the answer is yes, move on to the second question: 'Do I need the full service or would I get all the enjoyment I get from it with a lesser service?' For example, are you paying for five devices to be able to log into Netflix at any given time when actually having two logging in is more than enough, and cheaper. The added bonus of reducing five devices to two is that you will very quickly find out whether your ex is still using your Netflix!

18. Picking the wrong partner

I'm divorced. It's expensive.

I was so tempted to leave this one at that, but there is so much in this mistake alone that I could actually write an entire book on it. In simple terms, having the right partner is a game-changer when it comes to money and having the wrong one is a disaster. Before I go on, I am not saying that without a partner you can't be financially successful, but I don't think anyone single will disagree with me when I say that being single is much harder financially than being in a couple. Everything from single-room occupancy charges in hotels to being able to split rent versus paying it by yourself adds up over time and I recognise that. I also recognise that some people choose to be single. Singletons, I recognise your joys and your struggles, but all of us can learn from focusing on couples for a minute and the advantages of getting it right and disasters of getting it wrong.

When you and your partner are in sync financially, when you share the same goals, values and objectives, life just runs more smoothly. You are both pulling together to achieve the same thing, you can both be focused when you need to be and drive on. But also, nobody is perfect and nobody can keep the focus and drive that's required to achieve their goal 100% of the time. When one of you lacks the enthusiasm or energy for something, the other can pick up the slack. If one of you hits a bump in the road like redundancy or illness, the other can pick up the pieces for a period. You can support each other in these times, but it goes way beyond that. For somebody single every task, every move, every decision is on them. This suits some, but having a sounding board, a second opinion, from somebody who has skin in the game can not only result in better outcomes but it can simply take the weight off by diluting the burden of responsibility.

Even if you are not in sync there are advantages too when two different financial personalities come together. It can provide diversity, which can also result in better outcomes. All of this combined is evident in the research that finds that couples, on average, have a higher net worth than two singletons.

So when it goes right it can work out very well, but there is also scope for two people who are compatible in every other way to make an absolute financial mess of things. The opposite of being in sync and sharing common goals is not being in sync and neither of you having any direction. One person who is reckless with their own finances, racking up credit card debt, borrowing for everything, with no clue of what money they have or what money they owe can do serious damage to a couple's finances even if the other person is great with money. But when you have two people behaving like that it can result in things not just being twice as bad but becoming exponentially worse. If one person is out of control with their spending or lending or both and the other has similar attitudes to money, they either see the other person's behaviour as permission for them to do the same or they feel 'If they can do it, why can't I?' It is also often evident in couples like this that communication is poor and planning for their financial future isn't high on the agenda. Very quickly, and without resistance from either, a self-destructive 'borrow borrow borrow, we could be dead tomorrow' attitude sets in.

Whether it is two people making poor financial decisions or one person doing the damage while the other is trying their best, over time this can have an impact and can place strain on a relationship. When these strains start to show is often when I get called in. When I meet a couple for the first time I very quickly realise that the agenda isn't just about sorting out their financial future. I realise the person in the relationship who is carrying all the financial burdens is now feeling the pressure. They have tried to get the other person to mend their ways or even to take some joint responsibility for their finances, but they have failed and now they are turning, in this case, to me to see if I can get them both going in the same direction.

I am not a couples therapist but I am human and it is not hard to recognise what's going on. Typically when these couples present to me they often aren't so far gone that they, in my unprofessional opinion, need therapy. The step with me is often much earlier than that, and with a little direction from me and the right line of questioning the transformation can be magical. My goal in this circumstance is to find the thing or things about money that excite the rogue in the couple. Things that entice them to change their thinking and start to have a more positive impact. Sometimes it's about gamifying money or creating an environment where they recognise that a good financial plan will look after the long-term financial future so they can enjoy today financially guilt-free. Once they realise that all the anxiety around today's spending will be dealt with they often get on board with sorting out the long term. But what's most powerful in these meetings is actually where I give no direction, where I say nothing and the space is created for the couple to say out loud what's in their own heads about their current financial situation.

When things do go wrong in a relationship money is often the reason. 'We hit a tough time financially and things fell apart from there' or 'They leave me to look after the finances and then they swan around oblivious to our situation.' It may be that money caused all the problems, or perhaps the problems were there all along but simply got highlighted by the bank statements. Either way, when a couple are beyond the point of recovery it does serious damage financially. People think everything will be halved, they will each get 50%, but it is much worse than that. First, our archaic legal system is no longer fit for purpose; unlike other jurisdictions we don't have formulae or set rules to work out how to divide the assets. My simplistic view is that once you get to the courts it is about your legal team and their legal team going into a room together and coming out with a 'deal' that each team thinks they can sell to you and your ex and then hope the judge will sign off on it as fair. For me this process is littered with stresses, strains, emotions and problems and it is no longer up to the task. In a situation like this the court may split the assets 60:40 or 50:50 or come up with some other split based on circumstances, but often it is not the asset split that does the most financial damage.

You also have to consider that a family unit that once paid for one mortgage or rent for one home is now paying for two. Which also means two electricity bills, two heating bills, two bin collections. You are buying everything from your groceries to your Tinder subscription on the double now. You see, it is not just that your expenses are halved; each of you is now in the quandary we identified at the start of this section where we recognised that life is just harder financially for people who are single.

When I first started the divorce process somebody sat down with me and drew a simple picture – she had been through a divorce herself. She had sat down with her soon to be ex-husband at the start of it all and had this conversation

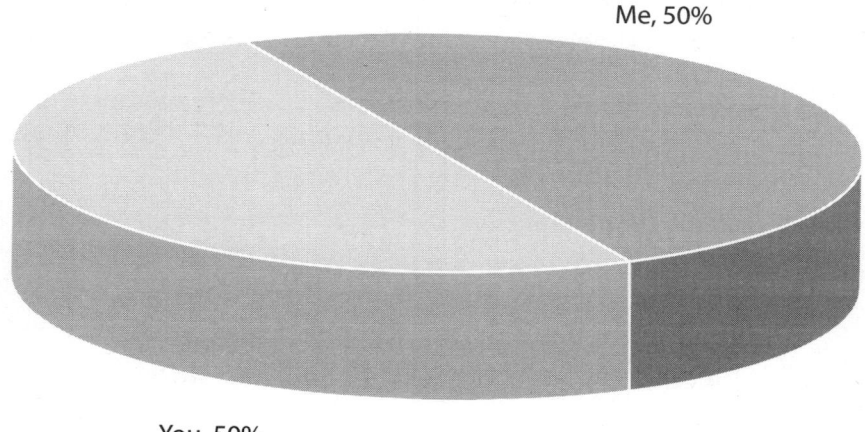

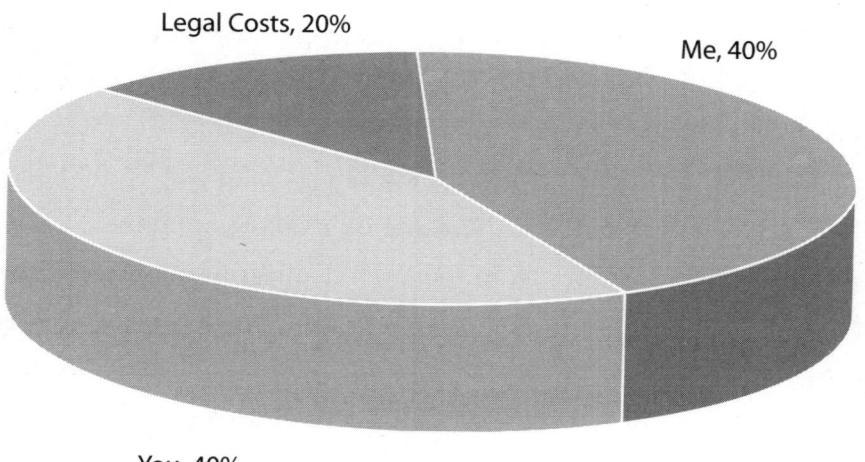

and it changed the dynamic of the split because it got them working together. She simply drew a circle on a page and drew a line down the middle and said, 'You think that this is how our assets are going to be split – 50:50.' Then she drew another line that took out a bite of about a fifth of the pie and explained, 'This bit here is for the solicitors and barristers. The more we fight the more they get and the less left for us', and, in their case, their kids.

I am not suggesting it was all sunshine and lollipops from then on but it certainly focused their minds at a time that was very difficult for them both.

I'll be honest, I'm not even scratching the surface here when it comes to couples and their money, but I think the basic point is valid. If you and your partner work well together financially it can more than just double your overall wealth and if you make the wrong decision it more than halves your overall wealth. The good news is that everything financial is fixable but sometimes the rest of the relationship has gone through too much and people part ways. So if you are in a difficult position and it's not too late, take action.

But if you are single or in a new relationship, consider this. We are all either exactly the same or exactly opposite to our parents when it comes to money. That doesn't mean we have to stay that way, but that is our default. Ask your partner what their parents are like with money and sit back and listen. You see, if you ask somebody about themselves a whole pile of barriers and protections kick in, but ask about somebody else and they will be less filtered and give you a real insight into their perception. From this description you will learn a lot about your partner's inbuilt beliefs about money and what they think is positive and what's negative and it's likely you will identify similar or opposite traits in your partner. This little exercise can give you a lot of advance warning on how life is going to be financially with this person. One word of warning – this isn't first date stuff.

Having totally sanitised everything that is love in this section I do feel I should end on a more positive note. Sometimes stuff goes wrong in life and it can seem there is no way out. But I believe when it comes to money and relationships everything can be fixed. Even when a relationship goes beyond the point of repair and you are in despair that things are never going to get better there is hope …

19. Not having a financial plan

When we go to the supermarket we bring a list. When we get in the car we open Google Maps. When we go on holidays we book, we research and we plan ahead. I could go on. In all walks of life we know it is the right thing to make a plan when we are doing simple, mundane things, yet when it comes to our personal finances many of us think it will all just work out in the end and we never bother to sit back and think out a strategy and then document that plan.

When somebody has a fear, it's often fear of the unknown. You are afraid of the dark because you don't know what's out there. You are afraid of needles because you don't know how much it will hurt. Even the randomness of thunder and lightning can be something that really scares people because they don't know what will happen next.

Time and time again money is identified as one of the leading causes of stress and anxiety and I would argue that part of the reason for that is the fear of the unknown. You don't know what you own, owe, earn and spend and you don't know where it is all going in the future.

By taking some simple steps and writing down your assets, your loans, your expenses and your income you take the first step of actually recognising your unknowns, which is your current financial situation. That's a great first step.

But by then deciding, and writing down, where you want to get to financially is when you really start to build your own personal financial plan. Once you know what you have and you can identify where you want to get to, it is just a case of working backwards from there to figure out the steps you need to take to achieve your goal.

You can definitely do this by yourself, but employing a good financial planner is the next step again. We will come back to this later, but people who have a good financial planner have 2.5 times the net worth of people who don't when they retire. Have a think about why that might be and we can revisit it later.

20. Deciding when to get into bed together (financially)

I have a guilty pleasure; I like *First Dates Ireland*. There, I've admitted it. I enjoy the drama, the human interaction and I get a strange second-hand embarrassment from time to time when people do something cringe or say something they shouldn't have. But it is the end of the meal that I really zone in on. I love seeing how the bill is handled. Who pays? Is it split? Or will one of them use the real smooth and really clever tester question, 'How about I pay this time and you pay the next?' This is clever because it means they get an immediate insight into what the other person is thinking about, whether there is even going to be another date and, more importantly, they get that insight before the camera is stuck in their face a few minutes later and they are asked 'Do you want to see each other again?'

It always fascinates me when people seem to get on really well on the date but then who paid, didn't pay or was willing to split the bill is a determining factor in whether there is a future to the relationship. It doesn't really wash with me that how the bill was split is the actual reason they don't see each other again, but it is a great excuse so the person doesn't have to open up about their real underlying concerns or problem with their date.

Sometimes I get bonus footage during the actual meal if they talk about money. But I think they should tread carefully here. Money is incredibly emotive and talking about it on a first date can create misconceptions of somebody before the other person has any idea of who they are. We have inbuilt senses in us passed down over years and years of evolution that basically mean we look for danger, particularly in new environments. Our ancestors may have been afraid of the wolf but remember, your date is trying to figure out if you are a wolf in sheep's clothing. On the other hand, their first impression of you might make them very interested in you. Or maybe they have had a long list of bad dates and desperately want this to work so they are zoning in on only the positive things you say.

Talking about money in any detail early on in a relationship is very difficult to navigate but can also be a lose–lose situation. For example, talking a lot about money can make you seem either very tight or very driven. If you don't talk about money, you might be perceived as being closed off or hiding something, or it might be seen as a sign that you must have lots of it.

If money does come up very early on in a relationship, I suggest that you engage but divert. You could ask 'What are your parents like with money?' or something more neutral, like 'What's the best thing you ever spent money on?' This often diverts the conversation away from money personalities and towards more emotional things like the holiday they spent money on.

I am not trying to be sneaky here; I just feel a first date is much more about getting to know the person before we label them as somebody who has loads of money or very little money – depending on how we categorise them based on what they say. We are all guilty of doing this to some degree, so everything I say about your perception of them is equally applicable to their perception of you.

If things go well and the relationship starts to blossom there will come a point where you do need to start talking about money. It is impossible to put a timeline on this because every relationship develops at a different pace. But you should be able to spot it. The first sign might be that you feel there is an imbalance because you pay for more stuff. Or, worse, you don't feel there is an imbalance, which probably means they pay for everything!

Couples can have an imbalance. That's perfectly okay, but it is only okay if there is open discussion about it. Anything in a relationship, particularly when it comes to money, will fester if it is not talked about openly. You have to establish that both parties are happy with how things are. This is true for spending, levels of savings and whether to have individual accounts, joint accounts or both.

When it comes to long-term planning you need to be together on this. You both need to be involved. If you don't decide together what the long-term plan is, when you want to retire, how much you are happy to put away each month, you are doomed to failure. It will be like you jumping into a boat and sailing off while your partner's at the end of the rope sitting in a rubber dinghy. Initially it might be okay – they feel comfortable, it's fun. But the first time a wave hits you, then you are on your own in the boat and you must go back to search for them. At best this delays your ultimate goal of reaching your final destination, or if the wave is particularly bad it might mean changing direction altogether.

21. Not saving

People say they aren't good savers. That's wrong. Nobody is 'bad' at saving. You are either in the habit of saving or you are not, making you either a saver or not. But everyone can save. Where people fall down is they think that the amount of money you save is really important. I would argue that it's getting into the habit that's important; you can worry about the amount later.

There are lots of obvious benefits to saving: when life happens you have money to call on; if there's something you want to buy you have your own money and are less likely to rely on expensive debt like credit cards or high-interest loans. But it also helps you keep up with your bills. One piece of research found that a little over one in ten people who don't save were behind on their bills; that figure was one in fifty for those who do save regularly.

The same research, by Bristol University, also looked at a group of people over a number of years and the researchers found a difference between savers and non-savers when it came to owning a home. They did six surveys, starting in 2011, and found that more than eight in ten people who had been savers in at least five of the six surveys were now home owners, compared to fewer than two in ten (1.5 people) who didn't say they were savers.

But the benefits of saving go far beyond just the financial ones. Research shows us that people with savings or who are savers suffer less financial anxiety and their overall wellbeing is more positive than those who don't save or have no savings. But the mind-blowing data for me was when it came to lower income earners; the impact of saving was more dramatic for them. Although having savings and being a saver is beneficial for all income categories, it was found that people in lower income brackets find being a saver more satisfying than those in higher income brackets. In fact somebody in a low income bracket who saved was found to be as satisfied overall with life as those in the highest income bracket who didn't save at all.

When you take a step back and consider the research, for me, it just feels like a real 'of course' moment. Sometimes having the research to prove what you know in your bones to be right or what feels like common sense just makes it hit harder. Of course, if you have savings you are more likely to be able to pay your bills, worry less about money and sleep better at night. And of course if you have less worry in your life your overall enjoyment of life will be greater. Add to that the fact that money worries are consistently, in poll after poll, in the top three of all worries and it isn't a big leap to realise that while alleviating any worry can improve your life satisfaction, alleviating financial worries can have an exponential effect on your enjoyment of life. It just makes sense.

But what it does highlight to me is that regardless of income, regardless of wealth, saving and having savings is the secret bullet when it comes to reducing our money worries and enjoying life more.

Other research shows that having just $500 in savings can dramatically reduce our overall financial stress. Let's just convert that to euros and use the figure of €500. Let that be your goal. If you don't save right now, set yourself a target of getting to €500. I don't care how long it takes you. You shouldn't either, for two reasons. The first is that you now know there are far-reaching benefits to saving. Second, as I said at the start of this section, you are either a saver or you are not – you decide. But if you decide to start and start at a level that is so small you make it impossible to fail, you will be a saver and you can turn up the volume of the amount you save as you go.

22. Not automating stuff

Making decisions is hard. It requires time, energy and willingness. Sometimes even emotion gets mixed in for good measure. When you can automate a decision it means you make the decision once, you automate it and then the only other time you have to decide something is when you decide to alter or stop the automation.

Take, for example, deciding to save. If you make a decision that when your next pay cheque lands you are going to save something, that's great. But what if you stop at that and then when your next pay cheque comes in you have to decide again to save from this pay cheque too, do you think there's a chance something might impact your decision? Maybe you think, 'Not this month, I've a wedding to go to' or a bill to pay or it's my pal's birthday. Or maybe you just forget. Whatever about sticking to your plan in month two, what's the likelihood that you'll stick with it month after month? Compare that to automating it.

You make a decision to save, you decide the amount and you

either do it in your banking app or you set up a standing order for it to happen each month. You have a much better chance of following through if this is the way you set it up because in a given year you make a decision once and stick to it as opposed to making a total of 12 decisions, one a month.

The same applies when you are stopping something. Life happens and from time to time you might need to stop your savings or your pension contributions. When you do this, automate the restart. Tell your pension provider that you want to stop for three months or six months or whatever. They will place a skip on the policy and after the defined period the policy will start up again. This means you won't need to remember in a few months' time to write to them to restart it. The reality is that when you stop something like savings or pension contributions, particularly after some financial shock like redundancy or illness, there will never be a moment where you say, 'Everything is great again now, I must start all my savings and pensions back up again today.' When you get a financial shock it does have an impact on your confidence and therefore will cloud your judgement as to when you are actually out of the woods financially.

Doing it this way takes the guesswork out of it and even after the elapsed time if you find you aren't actually through the worst of it then write to them again and put another skip on it. When these things are automated, it means that if you want to change it you have to act. And we know that we humans are inherently lazy and prefer to take the easy option even when it is not in our favour.

Auto-enrolment is a perfect case in point. Auto-enrolment works like this: when you start a new job you are automatically signed up to the pension. There's no paperwork, no hassle – you just join, and the money starts to come out of your wages. People not signed up to auto-enrolment have to sign forms to join the pension scheme, i.e. it is not automatic. Country after country have recognised that auto-enrolment is a good thing and that it encourages people to join pension schemes. The UK did it about ten years ago, and at that time about 45% of the UK's working population were in a pension scheme. Within a few years of auto-enrolment being rolled out that figure was closer to 85%. So it went from less than half the workforce having a pension to almost all of them. Why? Because they automated it and made it more hassle not to join than to join, so people just went with it.

Make your life easier – automate whatever you can.

23. Comparing yourself to others

We are coming to the end of the onboarding process and I have explained to the client that they are in great shape. We have identified their goals, the trips they want to take and experiences they want to have. We have looked after their loved ones. They have real clarity on where they are going financially and they have full confidence in not just their finances but also their plan. They had hoped they would reach financial independence within the next six to eight years and I have just told them they will be there in two years.

Then the question comes: 'How do we compare to others in a similar situation to us?'

I totally understand why they are asking this. It's a natural thing to ask, 'I think I am doing alright, but how am I doing compared to others?' Is it any wonder this is ingrained in us? Everything from my primary school teacher awarding a 'best person in the class' and an apple for being the best buachaill, to how the neighbours' kids' Leaving Cert results compared with ours, to who won the race on sports day, to who was voted most popular in school – it all leads us to ask ourselves how we compare to others.

But if you are living your best life, if you have a financial plan that achieves everything you want to achieve, if you can retire in two years instead of the eight you were originally thinking, does it matter where anyone else is at? Everything inside your door is perfect, so who cares what's happening behind someone else's door?

I totally get the question when I am delivering the opposite news, when I am telling somebody who thought they could retire in eight years that they can't retire for another fifteen. Questioning the position others are in is totally natural. 'How come they go on two holidays a year? And I know they earn less than us.' Or 'How come they get a new car every three years and I've been driving this banger for years? How are they doing that and I'm not and I can't retire for another fifteen years?' These are valid questions, but the honest answer is that nobody knows the full truth but the individual themselves.

Driving up from Cork a while ago I was listening to Nicola Tallant's podcast about the fella in Tralee who has been jailed for storing the largest stash of methamphetamine the country has ever seen. This guy had taken over the family business, a garden centre, some years ago, and the podcast described how he and his wife had done a kind of Celtic Tiger-era renovation, adding a restaurant, etc. They had more than one business, which appeared to be running incredibly successfully and providing employment to lots of staff. I actually met him and his wife once, the night their new burger joint opened in Ardfert in County Kerry. They were both working very hard on the night and for the few minutes I interacted with them they both came across as really nice people. They are incredibly well known around Kerry and appeared to have an amazing life. Going by pictures online, they attended loads and loads of events and were photographed with politicians and lots of other notable people over the years.

When Nicola Tallant and her co-presenter went through the facts of the case they revealed a very different story. In court it was said that the man did not have the business acumen to run the company successfully, and Nicola said he owed Revenue €2,000,000 in VAT and taxes. It was also believed that the €150,000 he was expecting to pocket for storing the drugs was to fund his lifestyle and not to clear any of his debts.

On the face of it these two appeared to have it all. They were a good-looking couple, attending fabulous parties and events and living a great life. But underneath it all they were smothered in debt and caught up with one of the most notorious and dangerous drug cartels in the world.

So when it comes to money, never judge a book by its cover. Just concentrate on you and don't worry about what others have, are doing or are spending.

24. Surrounding yourself with the wrong people – personally and professionally

We have already talked about how it's important to get advice, particularly online, from people who are qualified to give it and how it can blow up in your face if you follow the advice of the wrong people. But it is also really important to be surrounded by the right people.

We have all heard the adage that we are just a blend of the five people we spend the most time with. In other words we take bits of each of them, which influences us and forms us into the person we are. So we are an amalgamation of all our closest friends and family. That make sense to me because it's an observable phenomenon. Think back to your schooldays, when similar people hung around together – birds of a feather flock together. So maybe others influence us to become who we are, or maybe we are attracted to people who are similar to us because they resonate with us.

But if this is true, we must be careful who we decide to let in – who we are willing to let into our inner circle. I've always felt this is important, but recently I came across some research that really confirmed what I always believed. This was a workplace study. The researchers analysed the impact on participants of sitting within 25 feet of somebody who was considered a high-performing worker versus sitting the same distance from an underperforming worker. The study found that sitting near the positive influence resulted in participants' performance increasing by as much as 15%, but sitting near an underproductive employee resulted in performance being negatively impacted by as much as 25%. In simple terms, the negative influence had more of an impact than the positive influence.

Take that outside the workplace and think about what it means for you and your personal finances. If you spend most of your time with people who struggle with money, make bad financial decisions and don't seem to be moving forward financially, do you think that's going to be good for your wallet or bad for it? On the flipside, if you are surrounded by people who are go-getters, who discuss money with you and are overachievers, that will have a positive impact on you, but there will still be room for you to push on and achieve more.

But also think about what it means for society. If people in well-off areas and disadvantaged areas are so heavily influenced by their surroundings, how do we break that cycle for some and how do we share the advantage others have with everyone? That is probably a question for a politician to answer, but it is certainly something for us all to be mindful of.

Let's not forget that studies are not perfect and they work on pooling lots of data together and using averages to draw conclusions. You may not be affected in the same way as others by spending time with negative people, but you should be aware of it. Most important of all, life is about more than achieving financial success and any good friendship is worth its weight in gold.

25. Buying things, not time

If you want to use money to make you happy, don't buy things with it, buy experiences. If you go on an amazing life-changing trip this year, you will still remember it in ten years' time, but I bet you won't remember what version of your phone you had on that trip. Life is about experiences, not things.

Taking it a step further, one of the things common to people who are becoming wealthy or who already have wealth is their attitude to time. Whether we realise it or not, we can all make more money, but none of us can make more time.

However, having lots of money means you can actually buy time. Let me explain. Let's look at someone who has a trade – an electrician, for example. They work for themselves so all the income and of course all the bills belong to them. They are out the door busy, they just can't keep up with the work and they could be working seven days a week if they wanted to. Now, they need to paint the garden fence. They don't want to do it – in fact they hate doing it. But they have avoided doing the job and they know if they don't do it soon they are going to end up having to replace the fence because it will start falling apart. They plan on doing the job this weekend and they know they will get it done in one day, so if they start Saturday morning it will be done by the evening. On Thursday they get a call asking them to do a job on Saturday. They aren't sure what to do.

You might argue that they can't work all the time and they can't let their home be neglected. But what if we look at it differently? They look at the money they will get for the job on Saturday and they chat to a painter they were on a job with recently. The painter reckons they can get the job done in half a day and will charge our electrician less than what they are getting for the job on Saturday. Mathematically it makes sense for our electrician to avoid the job they hate, the painting, and do the job they are good at. Then they collect the money, pay the painter and will still be better off both financially and mentally.

This is a straightforward example of how you can buy time. In this instance our sparks uses the time to do a job that generates enough income to pay the painter and have some left over.

I see people who are comfortable financially doing this all the time. But they do it in a different way. They use the money to buy themselves time they can spend with their family or enjoy some other social activity or maybe just to have a lie-in.

A very simple example of this is the robot lawnmowers. I recently moved into a new home and it has a garden. I had a choice: spend a few hours in the garden every Saturday or get a robot mower. I got a robot mower, because I value my time more away from the garden than I would doing the garden; but I also want to have a nice garden.

Ask yourself what stuff do you do right now that, like our electrician, is costing you both time and money and what stuff are you doing that is simply costing you time, time you could afford to buy back and that would add value to your life?

26. Not naming your savings

Imagine this scenario. You are sitting at home on a Thursday evening and your partner arrives in from work and says, 'It's been a tough week, one day to go, come on, let's go out for dinner.' To which you reply, 'We have no money.' Then your partner says, 'We can take it out of our emergency fund, this is an emergency, isn't it?'

Now, rewind for a minute and let's play that back again but this time we will change one thing.

'It's been a tough week, one day to go, come on, let's go out for dinner.'

'We have no money.'

'We can take it out of our … weekend … away … next … August … Never mind.'

The only difference here is that the savings have an name. You had both sat down and called it something you both wanted to do together, and this meant that it had more meaning. They knew they were asking you to give up something you both decided you wanted to do together in order to go out for dinner tonight. The conversation shifted completely because you had created an emotional attachment to the money. It wasn't just an account number any more.

Most, if not all, banking apps these days will allow you to name your pocket, space, wallet, etc. whatever you want. It is a simple feature that is an absolute game-changer. Some of the more fuddy-duddy pension companies and investment houses haven't caught up with that yet, but they should because it makes us all think before we act. Imagine how many times you would think twice before dipping into Little Johnny's College Fund or the Money for the Honeymoon.

Emotion can misguide the financial decisions we make but it can also be used to our advantage.

27. Thinking more money will fix bad habits

I have already mentioned that I struggle with my weight. Well, back in 2008, when *Operation Transformation*, presented by Gerry Ryan, burst onto our screens, I was carrying a lot of weight, and this new show inspired me to do something about it. Over the next ten months I went from the couch not just to 5k but to running my very first marathon, 26.2 miles. Running that distance is tough and it requires a lot of training.

That training resulted in me losing a lot of weight. I felt great. I also felt I had discovered my secret to losing weight. If I continued to run, how much I ate, the amount of calories I consumed, the types of food I ate – none of it would matter. All I had to do was keep running the miles and not only would I not put on weight but I would continue to lose it.

How wrong I was.

The reality was actually very different over the long run.

Initially it worked a dream, I went from sedentary and eating too much to going out running and eating the same amount and the weight fell off. But eventually my body caught up and the weight stopped coming off. I was still running the same miles but at best my weight had plateaued. Then the inevitable post-marathon mileage drop-off hit and I had changed zero habits and all of a sudden the weight piled back on.

My solution? Sign up for another marathon. This time I would increase the mileage I did week by week. The weight started coming off again. It was working. Problem solved.

Wrong again.

I chased this for years. I ended up doing nine marathons over the coming years. They did become about more than weight loss. I got to run Dublin a few times, London twice, New York and, probably my favourite, the Connemarathon in Galway.

It was two weeks after London in 2018 that I banged my head, which, on reflection, was probably when I was at my heaviest. Even after ten years and nine marathons I still had not learned the true lesson of my weight-loss journey. Even though I was at my heaviest doing London, I still thought I knew what I was at. I was still telling myself that I was just carrying the weight because I hadn't done enough miles for London.

When I was forced into bedrest for months after my accident and I was not able to run, one of the decisions I made was around my diet. Over the next six months I lost a significant amount of weight – in fact, I was in the best shape I have ever been in as an adult – and all without being allowed to run a single mile. Why? Because I was doing what the experts say is the right thing to do. I was eating the appropriate healthy amount of calories, I was eating the right balance of food and I had a good relationship with food.

I tried to do it my own way. I succeeded, failed, succeeded again and the cycle continued. But in fact the expert knowledge was out there – the right way, the healthy way was known – I just chose to believe I had somehow cracked the code and discovered a better and, more important, an easier way to do it. The reality is that, whether it's your weight or your money, there are no shortcuts, there are no quick fixes or get-rich-quick schemes that work over the long run. It is about getting the right information from the right people who are qualified to give it and then applying it day in, day out. You have to put the work in; it doesn't have to be hard, but you do need to do the small things right repeatedly if you want big results.

I thought 'more miles, more weight loss'. But ultimately my issues with weight gain and the reasons behind it didn't go away because I added more miles. You need to accept the same with your money. If you have money issues today, unless you look at the root cause of those issues those problems won't go away if you have more money. In fact, if you have a small amount of money the money problems you have are small. But if you have more money the problems just get bigger. It's all relative, of course, and when you are in it the pain feels the same. But when eventually you step back and look at the numbers it can feel different looking at a credit card bill with €500 on it versus looking at a credit card bill with €50,000 on it.

At the end of the day you might think that more money means fewer problems, but it isn't true. No doubt we are all willing to give having more money a try! But the reality is that our relationship with money doesn't change if we make more of it or have more of it. The same way that running more miles might make you feel good for a time but ultimately you can't outrun a bad diet.

28. Thinking you will be happy when you have more money

It is not just that having more money won't magically solve all your problems; we also have to accept that having more money won't magically make you happy. If we're poor and miserable now I have no doubt we would be keen to try being rich and miserable, but there is often the assumption out there that having more money will all of a sudden make us happier. If you're struggling in life, having no money can both seriously aggravate that and pile on the anxiety you are experience. But the opposite absolutely is not the case – having lots of money won't make you happy.

We can draw on lots of things we have discussed so far, like the Harvard study that shows it's our relationships with other people that are the true source of our happiness, the fact that it is experiences, not things, that bring us long-lasting joy, and the experience I have had with lotto winners and people who come into 'new money' and their need to focus on the things that made them happy before they had the money because that is what will bring them true happiness in their new world.

These things are all valid and very true, but there is another damaging element to the mistake of believing that more money will make you happy, and that is that we often cover up the problems or lack of happiness in our lives today by blaming them on not having money. Also, when we hold this belief, that everything will be okay once I am rich, it robs us of the joy we have today. We miss all that happens along the way because we constantly sacrifice today in the belief that 'Sure I can't be happy until I am rich.'

By focusing on the prize we can strip ourselves of everything from now until then. As I write this I have just come out of a client meeting. It was one of those meetings that reminds me why I love what I do. It was much more about life and how the clients' money is going to support them and less about the technical stuff I have to do during my day job, which is important, but nowhere near as rewarding for me. These clients are in their mid-50s and have good solid careers. They have accumulated very decent wealth and are working away in their family business. They had just received some news – and if the meeting had been yesterday it would have been very different. Two days ago they lost a job that would have kept them very busy for all of next year. Then last night they replaced that work. Those are the ups and downs of working for yourself; and if you do it yourself you'll know the ups and downs all too well. This shock, which has since been resolved, meant the meeting took a different direction.

We spent the meeting looking at the numbers, looking at their long-term financial future and looking at when they would reach financial independence.

One thing that is very fortunate about the way we build our financial plans is that we are very conservative about all our 'guesses'. For example, when somebody is investing in a portfolio with 60% exposure to shares and 40% exposure to bonds we assume it will grow by 4.5% per annum. The fact is the portfolio we use with that split has actually done 7.05% per annum over the last 20 years (to the year ending 2024). You see, when we guess 4.5%, we know our guess will be wrong, but we are also confident it will be on the right side of wrong. If I guessed 8% and got 6% the client's financial plan would blow up. But if I guess 4.5% and get 6% the client isn't coming after me because they have too much money.

Being very conservative also comes into its own at times like this. These clients, based on our conservative assumptions, will be able to retire in three years' time because they will have reached financial independence. Due to the shock they experienced in the previous 48 hours, we decided to test their plan a little and see if we could get them to financial independence sooner than 2028.

Remember two things. First, we are conservative with our 'guesses' resulting in a conservative plan that everyone has confidence in. Second, these two have run their own business for years, they know life isn't linear, so they are prebuilt to try to work out where things could go wrong.

We played around with a few scenarios. First we checked

to see, if their investments and pensions were to grow by more than 4.5% per annum, how much they would need to grow so the clients could retire now. The answer was 7.47%, which is a little bit of a stretch but not ridiculous. Then we added one state pension (I'll explain later why we don't add in state pensions) to see if that made a difference, and guess what, it did! Then we looked at their current spending and worked out, if they retired today, what was the maximum they could afford to spend per month and not run out of money before their hundredth birthdays. They were pleasantly surprised with this number. We tried lots of other things, constantly checking with them as to how everything fitted together and what they were thinking might be around the corner that we were not allowing for, and then allowing for it.

It was a testing meeting. They really challenged their finances and looked at all avenues. It was brilliant. Ultimately they had pulled the figures apart so much and then put them back together again that they now had full confidence that if they wanted to give up work today they could and they would be okay financially for the rest of their life. We have only worked with these clients for the past few years, and this was their third annual review. They created the wealth – all we have done is put structure on it, but what they got from today goes far beyond money. They got confidence that no matter what is thrown at them, thrown at their business, they will be okay financially. They have made it. If they lose a client they will cope. Have a bad month, they will cope. Lose money on a job, they will cope. Stop working, they won't just cope, they will thrive and they have absolute confidence in their numbers.

Once they had confidence and they could see their financial future mapped out in front of them I then started to push them. You see, they have been working all their lives to create this financial security. They have enjoyed their lives, they are very happy together and have a lovely family. They have had fun holidays and experiences. They have not been hermits. But they have also now made a decision to keep working. The difference now is that they are going to constantly reward themselves. Even today they were talking about taking time off and going away. They have made a decision to put a gap between the next two big jobs they take on so they can take some extended time off and just practise retirement. They are doing this because, financially, they know they have arrived. They are working because they want to and not because they need to, so they want their reward now. It is no longer a case of 'I will do that when …', it is a case of 'When can I do that?'

This couple are an interesting example because they didn't hold back on their enjoyment of life, yet once they understood that today they are financially comfortable for the rest of their lives, their tone, their mood and their decision-making immediately changed and the future became now.

We could all take a leaf from their book and live more for today. We all need to enjoy the journey more, not just the destination. After all there is a chance life jumps up and bites us and we might not make the destination.

29. Thinking the future is bright

'I have never seen a bad set of projections' is what my bank manager said to me when I was presenting my business plan for setting up my first business. He was right: nobody sits down and makes a plan with the expectation that the future will be miserable. We need to believe the future is bright, it is built into us and it is important that it is. If we weren't optimistic we would never take risks, never progress and never evolve. It is built into our nature to become better and planning for a crap future would not be conducive to that evolution.

It is a good thing.

We do, however, need to be mindful of the flaws associated with a positive outlook bias. It can cause us problems financially if we don't foresee some of the trip hazards or obstacles that might get in our way. I don't want to turn us into a nation of negative thinkers, but I do want us to be mindful of the risks. If we always think the financial future is bright this can lead us down the path of making decisions based purely on that idea.

I believe this is why credit card companies do so well, they play into the fact that everyone thinks they can clear their balance next month because next month everything is going to be great financially. I had a robust conversation last Christmas with somebody who will remain nameless (you know who you are). They quizzed me on why I don't like credit cards. They used their credit card perfectly, cleared it in full each month and had never paid a single cent in interest.

I explained that in my experience about 85% of people don't do this and do accrue interest on a regular basis. And of the other 15%, fewer than 5%, in my experience, would make it all the way through life without slipping up. So although I accept that one in twenty people who have a credit card will use it properly for life I think those odds are awful. Think about it. Would you leave your job and launch a start-up business? I know people do it all the time but there is about a 5% success rate for a start-up, with 95% of businesses having to close down before they manage to secure their first round of funding. Or would you write a book without a contract with a publisher? There is between a 3% and a 7% chance of being published. Believe me, it takes time to write a book, so would you be willing to take the risk with a roughly 95% chance it won't be published? Again, people do write books and they do get published, but would you? Because people do use credit cards properly, but not many people. Most people would be much better served staying away from them from the start.

So I explained to this friend that although they currently sit in the 15% who are handling their credit card really well, when it comes to credit cards everything is okay until it isn't. It was Christmas, we were, let's just say 'relaxed', so the conversation went back and forth with neither of us feeling we had actually convinced the other that our point of view was correct. But I also felt that I had let them down because they didn't see my way of thinking and they felt they were in the 5%.

Well, last week I found out they didn't clear their card and had accrued interest for the very first time. Genuinely, I was not happy or smug or feeling anything but sad for them that the credit card crash had eventually hit their pocket and I do hope that once the card is up to date and cleared that they cancel it. I do hope this first-time lesson, coupled with the discussion we had, has been enough to show them that practically nobody is invincible when it comes to credit cards. We all think the future is bright and that's a good thing. But when it comes to loans, credit cards, buy now pay later, this positivity is used against us to entice us into making decisions because 'Sure I'll defo get me bonus next month.'

30. Thinking the route to financial freedom is to work harder

Work smarter, not harder is how the saying goes. There is something to that, but other than being born into money I honestly believe everyone's success does require some level of hard graft along the way. I don't think you can cheat your way to financial freedom. To avoid the hard work, you have to be either really lucky, really smart or both. For the rest of us, it will require hard work at least for some part of our careers.

But although reaching financial freedom can't be achieved without having some level of income that can be used to create assets, your financial success depends on two crucial things: how you manage your assets; and how much money you need to live your life.

If you were willing to move to some remote part of the world and live off the land you could probably retire today. All you would need is enough money to get you there and a small amount to set yourself up. Extreme as that is, it does highlight the fact that whatever it costs to live your life is a factor in reaching financial independence.

But equally, how you use the money you earn and the wealth you have created is important too. You could have somebody making loads of money, controlling their expenditure down to the last cent and yet the money they have is not being used correctly and therefore they are on what feels like a financial treadmill never really making any progress toward their goal of financial independence.

You work hard for your money, but does your money work hard for you?

Take child benefit as a perfect example. If you don't have kids, don't worry, I won't leave you out, the maths is just the maths. Child benefit is €140 per month. If as a parent you are lucky enough not to need that money and you can afford to put it away, where you put it matters. If you don't have a child but do have €140 the same maths applies to you!

If you put the €140 per month in a bank account and manage to achieve a deposit rate of 1% over 18 years (let's ignore tax, to keep things simple), it will mature at circa €33,000. But if you invest €140 per month and you get 4% growth, again ignoring tax, you will end up with circa €44,000. If the fund you choose managed to achieve 6% per annum you'd get just over €54,000 and at 8% it jumps to more than €67,000.

This is the same money being used in different ways and getting very different results. It highlights the need to get yourself into a position to know the harm leaving money in a bank account over long periods of time does; it highlights the need to educate yourself on where to invest; and it highlights the need to know how to invest.

Our financial life is littered with these examples: we do the wrong thing at the wrong time for the wrong reasons, and then we have to work harder to make up for the fact that our money isn't.

Outside influences

If we're honest with ourselves we can admit we all make mistakes, in all areas of life, not just with our money. But we all know people who genuinely believe they have never put a foot wrong in their life. In fact I know somebody who would have a full-on conversation with you telling you that black is white, and when things do go wrong it is absolutely not their fault, ever. In their mind they are faultless and the world is to blame for any misfortune. To be honest the person I am thinking about is probably quite unwell, but it doesn't make them any less convincing in their arguments, and if it is an illness they have they are blissfully unaware of it.

We all need to take responsibilities for our own actions and when we make a mistake we need to own it, because it is in the owning of it that the real learning is. But sometimes the mistakes we make are not all of our own doing. Sometimes there are outside influences guiding our decisions that we are unaware of but that can have real impact on how we behave and, to come back to the purpose of this book, can make us make decisions with our money that without these influences we may not have made.

I am not talking about mediums or psychics or some out-of-body experiences or other-worldly control here, I am talking about heuristics and biases. These are two different but interconnecting things and are studied in the areas of behavioural economics, neuroscience and psychology. This is a world that fascinates me and based on listeners to my podcast is an area that people really are interested in.

In simple terms, heuristics are the mental shortcuts we take just to get through life. Think back to the days we once lived in caves. You are out on an afternoon stroll and you stumble across a lion and they look hungry. Fight or flight? This is a heuristic. Your brain will assess the situation at lightning speed and make a decision to pick up that stick on the ground and fight or to leg it. It's a shortcut. Your brain will come up with a strategy very, very quickly based on the limited details available. This is why sometimes when we look back on a decision we've made we think 'Why did I do that? If only I had just sat back for a second and thought about it.'

Interestingly, it is easy to recognise when a heuristic kicks in when things go wrong, but it is less likely you will recognise it when things go right. That's the point. It is our brain taking shortcuts to get us through the day. Why would our brain have us question it if the brain made the right call?

This is simply learned behaviour and it is at play all day

every day in the tiny decisions we make continuously, decisions we are often unaware of even making. It is assuming a person in a hospital wearing a white coat is a doctor because they are wearing a white coat. Or you see a well-built bloke in a tank top and assume they are a gym bro, healthy and disciplined. Or, a perfect example, when I was at a conference in California we were staying in a little seaside town called Newport. There was a bakery there with a very long queue outside at 11 o'clock at night, so I assumed the food was good. It was open 24 hours so the next morning, at 4.30 a.m., when the jet lag had me awake, I got out of bed to go get what turned out to be quite a mediocre croissant. Maybe the people in the queue really believe they are the best ever or maybe they just haven't had croissants made with proper Irish butter!

Heuristics are our brain taking shortcuts, but these shortcuts are based on learned behaviour. They differ from instincts in that we are born with instincts, for example a baby instinctively grabbing a finger, but heuristics are developed over time, they are strategies that we build. We learn from past experiences and, rightly or wrongly, we use that learning again in the future, often to save time. If we didn't do this we would be trapped in a world of constant over-analysis which at worst would lead to paralysis and at best would leave us exhausted before we had finished our breakfast.

Heuristics can lead to biases, but not the other way around. A bias is often confused with a heuristic but, to simplify it, a heuristic is a tool or a strategy our brain uses; a bias is a tendency or pattern we follow. Unlike a heuristic, which is all about mental shortcuts, a bias is a systemic tendency that can sometimes distort our judgement. Imagine the scene: you are a Dublin football supporter on All-Ireland final day. Based on lots of little things – the weather, the feeling in the crowd and previous games against Mayo – you conclude, 'Dublin are going to win!' When Dublin do win (of course – this is my book, after all) you declare that you knew this was going to be the outcome all along. Actually, you didn't know all along; you took some very simple cues and guessed the outcome of a very complex situation. This is heuristics at play. The determination afterwards that you knew all along is what's called a hindsight bias, where your brain draws on a selection of the now available information in order to support your desired narrative.

Our biases can lead to poor judgements, but the good news is that you don't need a master's in behavioural economics to avoid them; you simply need to be aware that sometimes the mistakes we make are not all of our own doing. Sometimes companies take advantage of the fact that they have someone in their office who does have a master's in behavioural economics and can therefore use these tools against you.

So what do you need to be aware of and what can you do about it when you recognise it? Luckily, recognising it is significantly more than half the battle. Recognising what is going on means the conscious brain has kicked in, you are making more rational, thought-through decisions, and you are no longer on autopilot.

Let's look at several of the main things that you are likely getting caught out with every day but up until this point you may have been blissfully unaware of.

Price anchoring

One of the earliest jobs I ever had was in retail. I got a six-week temporary Christmas contract with a well-known high street jeweller's on Henry Street in Dublin. They were a large UK company with lots of shops across Ireland and the UK and I have to say their training, their policies and procedures and their thought processes and knowledge were well ahead of their time. These guys were using what they knew about biases long before many other companies in the world and certainly long before some of the other jewellers they were competing with on Henry Street had even heard of them.

When I was on my temporary contract, if somebody came in and wanted to look at engagement rings, I wasn't allowed to see to them; you needed special training to be allowed to 'advise' on diamonds. Mission accepted. I was one of a few who were offered a part-time role when Christmas was over and I was keen to get my De Beers training done so I could do the top job on the shop floor – diamonds. Funny how that was so important to me then; I'm chuckling now as I think of it, which ironically is skirting around the edge of another bias – hindsight bias.

Eventually I was offered the chance to do the training and it wasn't long before I was able to help people pick their engagement ring. A lovely thing about that job is nobody is ever in bad form when they're choosing an engagement ring.

The couple or the individual is full of excitement, anticipation and love, picking out something that they plan on having for ever to remind them that they chose to commit to each other.

At the time I loved it, but looking back on it now I do think the training was so good it was sneaky. If a couple came into the shop and asked to see the engagement rings we would go to the window and retrieve a tray, but it wasn't just any tray of rings – we were trained to pick the most expensive. You would bring the tray out and at that time, from memory, most of the rings were more than £10,000 (it was punts at the time). You would show them the rings and there would be some the couple – or at least one person in the couple – would immediately fall in love with.

Then the discussion around cost would come up and inevitably I would be asked if we had anything a little less expensive. What we were trained to do next was really interesting to me now: we would go and get the really cheap tray and put the other tray away.

There were a couple of things going on here. First, by putting the more expensive tray away you were narrowing down the decision funnel and by bringing out the cheaper rings costing about £300 you were now presenting the customers with these as the only option. The first were just too expensive, and these just looked cheap, so the brain looks for a solution and the final question comes: 'Have you anything at a price point between the two?'

That's when the £2,000–£6,000 tray came out and we would find something that suited them. I can't stress the number of times I heard at the point of sale, 'I really wasn't expecting to spend that much but we got the right ring.'

What happened here was price anchoring; I don't think I ever sold a ring from the expensive tray, nor do I remember selling anything from the cheap tray. The company knew they wouldn't be big sellers, but that's not the point; they were not there to be sold, they were there to create the anchor. Once you saw the first tray you anchored yourself mentally to that price point. When you are anchored to €13,000 for a ring, all of a sudden €3,000 doesn't seem that bad. Even though when you walked in the door mentally your anchor was €1,000 and you would never have imagined paying triple that.

Price anchoring happens all the time: the ridiculously priced steak so the expensive one doesn't seem that expensive. The small, medium and large fries where they are actually planning on selling you the medium. Or the 'was €100 but now €60' that's designed to have you anchored to the €100.

But did they get the right ring? I was young and this was how we were trained but looking back on it now I do have regrets about it. Did people, because of this sales tactic, spend more than they could afford? Did it stretch them too much? What did they go without? To me now looking back, I was one cog in a machine that pulled on so many psychological and emotional levers at a time that was a very happy one in their lives. Taking a male/female couple, how does a man look at his wife-to-be when her eyes are bright with delight and say, 'It's too expensive, put it back.'

I carry a lot of discomfort about the whole process now.

I have the excuse that I was young and impressionable and I thought this was the way the world worked. But I do regret it, I have for a very long time, because I think it was unfair. Thankfully it is a lesson I learned very early in my working life and it has guided many of the decisions I have made since about transparency, honesty and making sure my clients know all the good and bad associated with any products I am helping them to buy. In Prosperous we have four core values and one of them is 'Always do the right thing for the client even if it is not the right thing for Prosperous'. The entire team live by this. This core value didn't come out of thin air; it grew from my early career and me wanting to make sure that I and the team around me left our clients in a better position after our engagement (pun intended!) than before. We want to make sure, to the very best of our ability, that clients make the right decisions for their financial future and we want to support them in making those decisions. Having an entire team working with this ethos has resulted in amazing outcomes for our clients and the team have exponentially improved the financial future of thousands of people. Which is brilliant, but it still doesn't make up for how I feel about some of those early sales of diamond rings.

Scarcity

From diamond rings to Rolex watches …

Apart from stores on the high street, ('When they're gone, they're gone'), Rolex is the master of the scarcity bias. I have a friend who likes a nice watch and is a serious collector. He has built his collection over the last ten years or more and makes a lot of money selling some of his collection for a profit and using those profits to buy other watches, which he then holds for a few years before selling them on.

This world was new to me and so over a pint in Spain this summer he filled me in on how it works. This is my understanding. If you are new to the world of luxury watches this is going to fascinate you.

You can't just walk into a Rolex store and walk out with a new watch; that's just not how it works. You go in, you look at all the watches, if they think you're serious they might offer you something to drink, maybe even a glass of champagne. You try them on, the highly professional and knowledgeable member of staff explains the features of the watch in intricate detail and even tells you stuff you didn't know you wanted to know about watches. Overall it is a very pleasant experience, in beautiful surroundings, and it plays into lots of different feelings and emotions. But when you reach the point of actually buying, this is where it all changes.

You see, Rolex has mastered the art of creating demand by using scarcity. Once you decide you want to buy they check your profile on their system. If you don't have a profile you are already on the back foot and you will need to set one up with them. Then they add your name and the details of the watch you want to their waiting list and what happens next is … nothing. No deposit, no credit card details and no idea how long you will be waiting. They don't know what watches are coming in or when they will arrive. They get a delivery, open it, check what watches are in it and then go to their list. This is when it becomes hierarchical. If you are the only person on the waiting list for that specific watch you will get a call and you will have a certain amount of time to come in and buy it. But if there are others on that list they prioritise based on a black box of criteria that I believe are based on several factors, including your buying history.

I tested the 'other factors' recently. There are only three stores on the island of Ireland that are official Rolex distributors – Keanes in Limerick and Cork, Weir & Sons in Dublin and Lunn's in Belfast. I went to one of these stores to do some research for this book and enquired about a Rolex. The sales assistant recognised me from the TV and we had a bit of a chat. That's when I gave a little wink and a nudge and asked, 'If I buy this, can you get me bumped up the list?' (I'll stress this was purely for research purposes!) His response was incredibly professional. He just said 'No'. He was polite and he was direct. He explained they have a system and they stick to it. I pushed a little, and he explained that if he bumped me up the list and I met somebody also on the list and they asked how long I'd waited it could ruin the trust their existing customers have in the system.

This scarcity creates demand in itself, but it also creates a secondary market. People with money like expensive watches and people with money tend not to have to wait for things, so the secondary market for high-end watches is very strong. The secondary market is built on rich people who are prepared to pay over the odds to skip the queue combined with a large group of people who love these watches and go in search of ones they believe to be special.

How the secondary market works is like this. I build up my history with Rolex or Patek Philippe or some other high-end brand and I recognise a watch that is in demand now or I believe will go up in value on the secondary market in the future. I go and have my glass of champagne and put myself on the waiting list. When the watch comes in, let's say 18 months later, I go and buy it.

You'd think I would then just stick it up on the high-end watch equivalent of DoneDeal there and then, but that's not how it works. The watchmakers do benefit from the fact that there is a secondary market because people who buy their watches live in both the hope and the expectation that what they buy will go up in value because of demand. The demand which is ironically driven partly by the scarcity. But the watchmakers must also be careful about how the secondary market operates. It is part of the entire ecosystem that the watch brands have created collectively and they want to keep it alive. If I were to put the watch on the secondary market immediately after collecting it, it is no different from the sales professional bumping me up the list. Other watch collectors would find out that yer man Eoin McGee gets watches and sells them straightaway and thus deprives us true loyal fans from getting access. So, if you're seen to be offloading on delivery you go right down the pecking order on that waiting list. That same list that nobody really know how it works.

What I would need to do is go on the waiting list, wait, buy the watch, wait again and then at least 18 months later consider selling the watch. All this activity and all this waiting is creating scarcity, which in turn creates demand, which in turn, Rolex et al. hope, will drive up prices.

Not all of us are in the market for high-end watches, but that does not mean that we aren't affected by scarcity. Scarcity drives our purchase decision-making process more than we often realise. That slogan I mentioned earlier – when they're gone, they're gone – is a perfect example of a popular ad for a homeware store in Ireland and it feeds perfectly into the part of our brain that doesn't want to miss out. But it's not just people selling half-price homeware who use scarcity to get you to part with your money; it's used all the time. Think about the little note when you buy tickets for a flight that says, 'Only 3 left at this price' or 'closing-down sale' or 'limited edition'. These are all everyday examples of how we can be lured into spending because we think availability is limited.

Reciprocity bias

Have you ever been in one of the major cities in Europe and somebody who seems a bit down on their luck approaches you and gives you a free bracelet or some other gift? There are a couple of things at play here, and one is the reciprocity bias. They may also be blatantly scamming you and just trying to get close enough to pick your pocket, but let's park that for the moment. Focusing on reciprocity, what they are doing is playing into the fact that when somebody gives us something, particularly if it's free, we feel obliged to return the favour or help them in return, even if we don't want the thing they gave us.

It happens to us all the time in very simple ways as we go through our day; for example, the need we feel to say 'Thanks' when someone holds the door open for us is reciprocity bias. If you don't think it's real, the next time someone holds the door open for you try not saying thank you. I bet you will feel a strange pang of discomfort or awkwardness. That feeling is physical and it is real and powerful. Now imagine company bosses sitting in boardrooms trying to figure out ways of playing into this feeling you have in order to get you to part with your money.

When the Rolex guy gave me the champagne, that's because I would then feel obliged to pay him back. When you are given a free sample, or when a charity sends you a gift in the post, or even when an influencer gives you a free tip online before they try to sell you something, it's all reciprocity in action.

Like all the biases, it's often enough to simply be aware of them in order to either dampen down their impact or to make sure you think twice before accepting something for free.

Commitment bias

Getting stuff for free from businesses is often tied in with being a loyal customer. For example, I do lots of travel and I use Aer Lingus a lot. I'm a member of their loyalty programme, which means that I get things like lounge access, fast track, priority boarding for 'free'. This is playing into reciprocity but it's also playing into commitment bias, which is sometimes called consistency bias. It's where we choose one product over another because we have pledged some level of commitment to them. It can involve signing up to a loyalty programme, but it can also be as simple as 'I get my coffee there because I always get my coffee there.'

It also crosses over with brand loyalty. The definition of brand loyalty is where you will choose one product over another of similar quality even though the one you choose is more expensive. You do this because you are loyal to the brand or committed to the brand.

Commitment bias is very important to brands. It will be no surprise to you that companies know it is much more expensive to attract a new customer than it is to keep an existing one, so they go to great lengths to try to get you committed. Where they can, clever companies will remind you of positive past experiences, your belief that they are prestigious and reliable; but they strike gold when they can get you committed to them as a result of an emotional connection.

Although there isn't the same level of science at play, at its simplest level this is about your local barman who makes you feel welcome every single time you come in. Or the person who works in the dry cleaner's remembering the reason you had to get your good suit dry cleaned in a hurry recently. There are lots of biases at play here, one of which is getting you to develop some level of commitment to that business.

When you consider the fact your barman can stumble across these powerful brand-building biases, imagine how much they are impacting your daily life when they are being used by people with big budgets and extensive education in the field.

Endowment effect

In late 2025 some research was done on the UK property market, specifically around the difference between the price at which a house is listed for sale versus the price it actually sells for. There has been a decline in the number of buyers for homes in the UK: in November 2021 there were ten buyers for every one home listed for sale; in August 2025 there were four buyers for every one home.

This drop-off has meant there has been an increase of 44% so far this year (2025) in the number of properties whose sale price has had to be reduced in the hope of selling it. In other words, the seller asked for too much initially, the property didn't sell, so they reduced the price. Estate agents in the UK have reported reductions of 15–25%.

When you list your property for sale and are forced to reduce it to try to move it along, the research says it takes 64 days longer and there is an increased likelihood it will not sell at all. There are a couple of things at play here. First, people who have decided they are not going to buy the property at the higher price have gone through the thought process of whether or not they want it. If they could have afforded it at the higher price, there must be other reasons why they don't want it. These reasons become entrenched in their minds and for lots of people these reasons don't vanish because the price comes down. The second thing that can happen is that somebody sees the price has been dropped and then they throw a low-ball offer on it because they think the seller must be desperate to sell.

Valuers in the UK say that it is actually quite easy right now to get an accurate valuation on a property before putting it up for sale, so you have to ask how this could be happening. Why would people go against the advice of the selling agent and push for a higher listing price? There are actually lots of reasons for this, one of which is loss aversion (which I will tackle in a minute); emotional attachment is another; but a key factor in all of this is the endowment effect.

Emotional attachment and the endowment effect cross over quite a bit, but basically they come down to the fact that we value something we own more than we would value the same thing if we didn't own it.

Think about your own home. If somebody asked you how much you think it is worth you might say something like €500,000. But if you didn't own the house and you were considering buying it, you are likely to value the very same home for less, simply because you don't already own it. Try this with your friends the next time a house sells in their estate or their road. Ask them how much it sold for and wait to see how they immediately start to explain why it went for less than their house is worth. It typically starts with something like 'Yeah, but they don't have a south-facing garden' or 'Their back garden is smaller' or 'The bathroom isn't done up like ours.' They aren't actually trying to convince you; they are justifying their own thoughts to themselves. They value their home at more than what the other one sold for and this is simply because they own it.

A famous piece of research (famous in my world, anyway) was done on this in 1990. Three behavioural economists, Thaler, Kahneman and Knetsch, split students into two groups. The first group were given mugs for free and the second group were given no mugs. The first group were then asked how much they would sell the mug for and the second group were asked how much they would be willing to buy a mug for. The sellers wanted double what the buyers were willing to pay for the mug. Think about that for a minute; these students were given a mug for free and immediately asked how much they would be willing to sell this free mug for. For me this illustrates just how strong the endowment effect is and for you it is something you need to be very aware of. Even if it is just to save you frustration the next time you go to sell your car and are insulted by the trade-in value you are offered.

Loss aversion

Loss aversion often explains some of the elements of the endowment effect, but they are different. One key difference is the fact that for the endowment effect to apply you need to own the item, but loss aversion can encourage different behaviours even when you don't own something.

Loss aversion is based on the fact that the pain we feel from a loss is far greater than the joy we experience from a win. The simple example is gambling. The pleasure from winning €50 does not feel as bad as the hurt we feel from losing €50, even though the amounts are the same. This often results in the gambler doubling down to try to chase the big win and erase the pain felt from the loss.

Some of our clients, at their annual review, say 'I'm not really happy with our investment and how it's performing. It doesn't really go anywhere, it seems to go sideways and it feels like it might even be losing money.' Then I show them a chart from the last few years and it clearly shows where they started and where they are now, and it is hard to argue that it isn't making money. Then I ask, 'Are you looking at the app regularly?' and the answer is always yes. What's happening here is that they are looking at it too often. With our style of investing, and using 100 years of data, a client in a mid-risk-level portfolio has a 75% chance of a positive return over one year, an 85% chance of a positive return over three years and a 99.6% chance of a positive return over five years. However, if you look at this exact same portfolio every day there is a 44% chance that compared to yesterday you will be down. The pain of 'losing' 44% of the time has far more impact than the joy we get from winning 56% of the time, so the individual carries that pain with greater weight and believes that their investment isn't moving forward.

But loss aversion applies in lots of parts of our lives. For example, when I rent a car I usually buy the extra protection.

This is because I know the pain I will feel if I clip a curb. That pain will last, I will worry about it until the entire thing is sorted and I know exactly how much it is going to cost me. So when I am buying the extra protection I am imagining damaging the car on day two of a six-day trip and I am accepting, because I know myself, that I will spend the last four days of the trip agonising over what has happened. I will constantly look at the damage. My brain will constantly be assessing all the different possible outcomes and will go wild with what the financial cost might be. For me, it would ruin the last four days. So for me the extra cost of the insurance doesn't just buy me peace of mind for the cost of the repair, it helps me avoid the loss of the last four days of my trip. This summer Clara and I rented a car in Spain. Driving through Seville we stopped for lunch and went into an underground car park. I curbed the wheel and did some damage. Of course I was annoyed with myself but I got over it very, very quickly and it did not spoil the rest of the trip. Why? Because I had cover for it and I had used this car hire company before so I knew when I dropped the car back that because I had cover they wouldn't even check the car for damage. There was going to be no stress, no haggling, no hassle.

Whether it is buying insurance, holding on to a bad investment for too long because you don't want to lose money, or leaving money that should be invested in a deposit account instead, loss aversion is intertwined in our lives. Recognising it and looking for situations where it is impacting you is very useful. I have a close friend whose therapist regularly challenges them on this: 'Are you not doing that out of fear or because you actually don't want to?' My friend has often changed decisions because they recognise that not doing something simply because of fear is not a reason not to do it. There may be other factors, and fear is one of them, but more often than not, whether it involves money or life decisions, if fear is the only reason we are not doing something it usually isn't a good enough reason.

Primacy bias

The first piece of information we get about something has more impact on us and helps us form our opinions more than information we get later. This can impact a trial jury's opinion, for example; the first piece of information quickly leads them to form an opinion and that opinion might be harder to change later on than it otherwise might have been. This is because the opinion has, to a degree, become ingrained. But it also has impact in things like job interviews, where the interviewer forms an opinion at the start, and then other biases, such as confirmation bias, can kick in to confirm they are right.

Primacy bias is also important when it comes to speeches. I have worked hard on writing the opening lines for my public speaking and corporate engagements. For example, one I often open with is the first line of this book – 'Beep … beep … beep'. It was scary to do it the first time. It's really important to get the pause between beeps right, but if you keep going, by the third or fourth beep you have the room's attention and people are intrigued ('Has he lost his mind or is this intentional?').

I say it usually grabs the room's attention, but once it didn't land at all well and all I could do was laugh. You see, on my second beep, the MC who had just introduced me interrupted me before my third beep could come out and said 'I am so sorry, Eoin, I don't know what those beeps are. Just give me a second to try to fix it.' Thankfully the room knew it was me making the beep noises and we all laughed together. What I am trying to achieve in those opening seconds is to get the audience engaged, interested and intrigued about what is to come over the next 45 minutes or so. If I can successfully get the room on board in the first 60 seconds it can be powerful and, for me, it feeds me an energy that is right up there with the best feeling I get from my professional life. I love it.

When we were still living in caves we had to be able to think on our feet and primacy bias enabled us to form an opinion quickly. We have evolved somewhat since then, but we still use this bias in lots of different situations. Have you ever met somebody, formed an opinion on them and then later found you were wrong about them? Maybe you had a very positive opinion about them and later they did something completely out of character and you were left stunned because you really thought 'they weren't like that'.

Sales people use this bias to their advantage. Next time you are being sold something, whether by a billboard or a salesperson, be very mindful of the first piece of information they offer you. For example, a clever car salesperson knows their audience so if they have a car to sell and see a young energetic prospect walk through the door with a motorbike helmet in their hand they might describe the car as 'fast, sporty and good value for money', but if someone middle aged walks in wearing a suit and carrying a briefcase they might make an assumption that they are more conservative and describe the car as 'good value for money, sporty and fast'. They are the same words, just in a different order, but the salesperson knows what word they want to be landing in their prospect's mind first. They know what buttons to press.

Also watch out for it watching an ad on TV, in a supermarket, online or on the back of the bus. What does the person selling this product want you to see first? Does the fact that you now recognise this tactic change your opinion of the product?

Primacy bias is intricate but it can be simplified. The most simple explanation is something your mother may have said long before the smart behavioural economists recognised it – 'First impressions last.'

Recency bias

The opposite of primacy bias is recency bias. This applies to the information we get last. Recency bias is a big part of the reason that back in 1997 Irish media were prevented from reporting on an election in the last 24 hours before the polls opened. Well ahead of its time, the thinking was that something that happened in the last 24 hours could adversely affect somebody's thinking and therefore change how they might vote. In simple terms, the last piece of information and the first piece of information we get about a topic or person carry more weight than the information we get in the middle. Broadcasters scrapped this practice in 2024, but that was more a recognition that the media and the world have moved on and although mainstream media might be under a moratorium you couldn't stop chatter on social media, for example, so if there was something significant circulating online the mainstream media could not report it and confirm the chatter was either true or false.

From an investing perspective, recency bias can be dangerous. I once took on a new client who had a pension with one of the big pension providers. When I reviewed it I was very confused. They had had this pension for more than ten years and they were barely above break-even; the value of the pension was only slightly higher than the amount of money they had paid in. This made no sense to me. It had been a really strong ten-year period, and I would have expected them to be somewhere between 60% and 80% up on their investment.

I asked the client how their previous adviser had been advising them to invest. The answer I got was a perfect example of recency bias doing a lot of damage. They explained they hadn't heard from the person who set the pension up for years, so they decided they would manage it themselves. They went on to explain their investment strategy. Each month they would log on to the website of the pension provider and review the performance of all their funds for the previous month. They would then move all their money into the best-performing fund, thinking that if the most recent information suggested this was the best fund it must be true. Their strategy had done significant damage to their wealth, but it had also resulted in the client thinking 'Pensions are useless.' Thankfully this client was young enough to recover and we spent a lot of time with them driving home the message that you set it up right at the start and you invest and forget. They are in a great place these days. In fact, I recently did their annual review with them and this client – in their early 50s – has reached financial independence. They are now working because they want to and not because they need to. But it could have been very different for them had we not fixed that one recency bias trap they had fallen into.

Recency bias can affect our investment decisions, but it is also present in good and bad financial times. For example, if you get hit with an unexpected big bill you become over-cautious with your spending in the expectation it is going to happen again. Or you get a big bonus and you spend it, thinking that the big bonuses are just going to keep on coming, because sure they have before.

The way to counteract recency bias is, like most of the biases, to recognise it. But with this one, trying to think long term can dramatically reduce its effect. Rather than budgeting based on what happened last month, budget based on what happened in the last year. With investing, go longer again; rather than last year, start thinking the previous decade. Think beyond the now and try to imagine the long-term past and the long-term future.

One key tool you have for recency bias is the 72-hour rule and you already know all about that. Don't buy it now, put it back, let the recency bias dissolve by waiting 72 hours.

Framing effect

Framing is incredibly powerful and leans into lots of the other biases we have discussed. This is where marketers and sales people know that our brain quickly frames something in order to decide if it is a good thing or a bad thing. Clever people can play into our thought processes to get the outcome they want.

For example there is a restaurant in the UK that offered certain regular customers a special key ring. This key ring entitled the bearers to roll a dice at the end of their meal and if they got a six they got the entire meal for free. This is genius because it plays into so many of our biases: endowment (we own the key ring); reciprocity (we are getting something for free); commitment (we are recognised and rewarded for being a loyal customer); even loss aversion.

For the restaurant it was a no-brainer. There was a one in six chance that any given table would roll a six. Provided that customer came back six times and only won once every six rolls that would be the equivalent of a 16.66% discount. But when you consider it across all the tables in the restaurant, it is statistically unlikely that the restaurant is going to get caught out on any given night. If each table has one chance of rolling a six, a quick google tells me, assuming there are 20 tables the statistical probability of every table getting a six in one night is 2.74 in 10 quadrillion or 0.000000000000027351 chance. (There are 15 zeros before the 2!)

This is a great example of framing. Think about being told 'Here's a special key ring that gives you 16.66% off'. It doesn't have the same impact, excitement or thrill as 'Here's a special key ring that allows you to roll the dice for a chance to get your meal for free.' At your table it is going to cost the restaurant either 16.66% or nothing, and there is an 84% chance it will cost them nothing. Yet it is invaluable when it comes to buying your loyalty and some free publicity.

It's not just clever restaurants that do this. We know that '90% fat free' is more appealing than '10% fat'. Even when it comes to marketing painkillers, research has shown that branded painkillers are actually physically more effective than non-branded ones because your brain tells you, 'You don't have a €1.20 headache, you have a €4.50 headache.'

Framing has also been shown to affect not just how we spend money but also how we taste things. I saw a documentary a very long time ago in which the same dish, cooked by a Michelin-star chef, was served in three different settings.

The first was a local café, which was clean but not very plush. The food was served with worn cutlery on plates that had seen the inside of a dishwasher a few times. People sat on steel chairs at tables draped in plastic table covers.

The second venue was a middle-of-the-road, good neighbourhood restaurant. Clean, presentable and with nice cutlery and well-presented tables. Overall the setting was comfortable and inviting.

The final venue was a top-end fine dining restaurant where every little detail had been considered, from the ambient lighting to the music, the best of crockery, the amazing art and excellent white-glove service.

Remember, the food was identical, just served in three different settings on three different types of plate. The documentary found that people rated the food depending on the surroundings; this is a classic example of framing. Charles Spence, an experimental psychologist at the University of Oxford, has studied this and has found that even things as simple as the weight of cutlery can change our perception of the same dish.

Knowing about the framing effect is great, but once you recognise it it is actually one of the easiest biases to counteract. To determine whether framing is inadvertently impacting your thought processes, one key trick is to flip the frame. So when you see a claim that says '90% success rate', ask yourself if you're happy with a 10% chance of failure. Another trick is if an ad for a €50 item says 'Save €10', ask yourself if you're happy to spend €40. Finally, ask yourself, 'What am I actually buying here?' instead of accepting what is being sold.

Social proof trigger

I hope that in the early days after this book goes on sale it hits number 1 in the charts. Why? Because it means we can put a 'No. 1 Bestseller' sticker on the book while it is on the shelves. Does this make a difference? Yes, it does. It makes a difference because of what's known as the social proof trigger. Most people want confirmation that what they are doing is the same or similar to what everyone else is doing, so that sticker would confirm to a potential buyer, 'It's okay to buy this book, sure loads of people are, it's a bestseller.'

Social proof is particularly powerful if we are uncertain about something we are about to buy. Oftentimes it doesn't just help us to choose, it influences us to make purchasing decisions, for example if we see a good Google or TripAdvisor review, or if we are told seven people booked this in the last hour. But we are also pushed along the buying cycle when we see testimonials or things that really join the dots, like 'Seven of your contacts use this app.' It is easy to understand this when we consider the phrases 'There's strength in numbers' or 'The more the merrier'; we like to feel part of something or, and perhaps more important, we don't like to feel out on our own. Feeling that we're part of something makes us more comfortable and confident, not just in our financial decisions but about many things in our life.

> Before I go on, and because of the specific topic we are discussing here, I want to declare that I have done work with the CCPC (Competition and Consumer Protection Commission) in the past and they have sponsored TV shows that I have presented, but they do not know about and I am not being paid for what we are about to discuss. (The CCPC is an independent statutory body that enforces competition and consumer protection in Ireland.)

Never before has the social proof trigger been more evident – and some might even suggest more powerful – than as a result of the rise in the use of social media. The suggestion that it might even be more powerful is based on my belief that many people don't realise it is in play and are totally unaware that they are being influenced to buy something. A piece of research done by the CCPC found that in general people had a negative opinion of the term 'influencers'; in fact, in the focus groups organised by the CCPC, the majority of people did not follow influencers. Rather, they referred to the people they followed who were influencers as 'people of interest' or 'interactive celebrities'. Not only that, the people in the focus groups did not really agree that these terms and the term 'influencer' were interchangeable. But the groups also showed signs of being unable to identify influencer marketing material. Despite the fact that 77% of people felt they would be able to recognise when they were being sold to or influenced by a post, when they were shown material that was doing just that it caused them confusion as to the nature of the actual post.

In simple terms, there is some suggestion that as a nation not only do we struggle to even recognise who the influencers are, we also struggle to identify when these people are selling to us. But does that matter? Yes it does. Two out of three people in the survey admitted they had bought something because they had been influenced by someone online. I don't blame them. You get an insight into someone's life that you either share a social circle with, for example because they played for the football team you've supported all your life, and you and they are part of the same tribe. Or maybe they aren't in your tribe but they are part of a social group that really appeals to you and you want to be part of. It is easy to see how these people can have influence on you; you see their life, you are either attracted to it or connected with it and they are using a product or service and you think that would suit you too because you are either like them or want to be like them.

The problem that buying something as a result of being influenced is that it doesn't always work out well. When we buy something the old-fashioned way, where we do our own research and maybe go into a shop and touch, feel and mess about with a product, it is reported that about one in twenty times we feel we have been misled in some way about the product we ended up with. But almost one in four people (24%) reported that they felt misled after buying a product as a result of being influenced.

I don't want to be totally negative about influencers – they often serve a really good purpose. When I am buying something it is useful to know a real person has tried and tested it. It is often helpful to see it being unpacked to get a sense of the quality of a product and watching it being used can give you a real feel for what the product is actually like; and if I can build up a level of trust that what I'm being sold is actually what I need it can save me a lot of time. But like many things in life it is often the actions of a few that damage the reputations of many. There are both good and bad influencers out there.

We just need to be aware of our own weaknesses when it comes to being influenced. For example, we often fail to identify an influencer, we struggle to recognise when we are being influenced, and when we buy stuff that we were influenced to buy we are five times more likely to feel we have been misled than if we bought it the old-fashioned way.

A simple and important tool that can help you navigate this entire field is the #. When somebody is selling you something, or is being paid to post something, they must use a #, for example #ad or #gifted to let you know that this isn't just their opinion. This applies to everything, including if they mention a business they own. For me this initially caused some confusion. I work on the premise that everyone who follows me online knows I founded and am the majority shareholder of prosperous.ie, or at the very least they know I am connected to it somehow. So when I was answering questions online I wondered whether I should add #adownbrand. It was particularly confusing when it came to things like people saying they had engaged with Prosperous and were complimenting the service they got from the team. When I went to share that, I would be wondering, am I actually selling something here or is this just information? Do I need to add the #? But when I saw the research and, more important, realised the impact influencers have (and often unbeknownst to the people being influenced) I made the decision that when I didn't know if I needed a # or not I was absolutely going to put one in. So if I was in doubt it went in. This isn't perfect and sometimes comes across as a bit odd, for example if someone says, 'Prosperous are great!' and I respond with 'Thanks #adownbrand' it just seems a bit strange. But ultimately it is the right thing to do. I want to protect the consumer and I believe the consumer would be much better protected if everyone online who had something to sell used the # properly. But unfortunately the reality may be that they know they sell less when they do it right.

Community trigger

We are tribal, and we often belong to many different tribes. When I walk into Croke Park and see the sea of blue I feel I belong. When someone goes to a book club they feel surrounded by like-minded people.

It can make decisions easier if we don't feel part of the tribe. For example, right now I am planning on leaving my golf club and looking for another. I only started playing golf two years ago and the club I joined is fantastic. The course, the facilities, the staff are at the very top end of what golf is in Ireland. I do love the place. But I've made very few friends there. Don't get me wrong, I've met some people whose company I really enjoy, and I've loved being around them and hearing about their lives and what they have going on. Some of them have become friends, but not that many. But ultimately I did not have the time to invest in becoming part of the tribe down there. As a rookie golfer I am realising that the club is an incredibly strong and incredibly inviting environment, particularly for newbies. But if I don't have the time to actually be in the club it doesn't matter how good the people in the club are, it is impossible to build those friendships. What's disappointing for me is that while

I've made friendships with some of the people there, I just haven't enough of those friendships to feel I am part of the tribe. I recognise this is entirely my fault and part of me feels disappointed that I didn't invest more of my time in the place because that club is at the top of its game and the people I have met there are fantastic.

But when I moved house this year it meant that club in Kildare is now over an hour away in good traffic and it is just too far away. Even if I did suddenly have a whole pile of free time on my hands the distance would still be a barrier. Somebody said to me recently that the best golf club in the world is the closest one to you, and this is very true. So I have decided I will try and get into a club locally and I will invest my time in a club that I hope will be my club for life.

My decision to leave one of the best clubs in Ireland was made easier because I felt I wasn't part of the tribe. If I did, lots of the other biases would kick in; for instance confirmation bias would tell me 'It's only an hour' instead of 'It's over an hour', and I might make the effort to stay.

An example of the opposite, for me, is the running club Clara and I belong to. Andrew Moore, aka the Fitness Goose, has created a tribe like no other. But he has done it in a way that recognises that people who run often do the vast majority of their runs alone and they do it alone because they can choose a time and place that suits them. Few other forms of exercise give you the freedom that running does in terms of its accessibility, lack of need for equipment and literally a world full of choices as to where you do it.

Andrew has used technology and in-person activities to create a tribe. He has a WhatsApp group for the entire club, which is very active and engaging; even smarter, he has also set up lots of different subgroups. When Clara and I were training for the Boston Marathon in early 2025 he put us into a Boston Marathon Chat months in advance with other people from the club who were also going to Boston. This created a little subtribe within the bigger tribe and made us feel part of something. Then it became self-perpetuating. Andrew throws in comments regularly but we are all also chatting among ourselves. When we were in organised group training runs we were engaging and forming friendship with all the other club members – or Geese, as Andrew calls them – but we were also acutely aware of looking out for fellow Bostonians. When we travelled to Boston we kept an eye on each other, checked in to see how people were getting on, made suggestions for things to do around Boston, because after all these people were part of our tribe and if we liked something they probably would too.

In recent months, while I have been writing, my running has progressively fallen apart, yet I remain a member of the group. Why? Because I feel part of something and although I am not utilising it the way I should be, and although I am most likely frustrating the hell out of Andrew, who keeps building schedules for me that I ignore, I know that when the book is done I am going to want to go back to running again. I know I have a tribe who will be accepting of me and I know I will get something from it.

You need to be aware there are people in the commercial world who have spent years perfecting the community trigger and they use it all the time to get you to spend, not just once but repeatedly. If they're really successful they will even get you to spend more than you would have without their work. They aren't evil, and I don't even dislike them; the opposite, in fact, I have huge admiration for the successful work they do. But I do feel we are all involved in this game and some of the players don't even know the game exists.

As with all the biases, there is some crossover, for example with the social proof trigger. But recognising the difference can help you navigate it if it is being used to simply get more money out of your pocket. The social proof trigger is about awakening something in you that gets you to buy something or do something because someone else has provided 'proof' that it is worth it, whereas the community trigger is about you doing or buying something because you want to be part of something.

You won't be surprised that I think recognising community trigger is the first step to tackling any negative impact it has on your personal finances. There are lots of positives and often community is what life is all about, but these community vibes go well beyond golf and running clubs. Community trigger is why somebody sticks with an Apple phone for years, ignoring any suggestion that Samsung might be a better option. It is the reason people spend big on a night out or buy expensive clothes; it's because that's what their social group does. It can be the reason you change your car or even house to keep up with the Joneses.

There are some key tools you can use to assess whether what you're doing is actually adding value to your life or if you are doing it just to 'fit in'. Having a plan is the first one. When you have a financial plan, decisions are easier, but it also gives you more clarity on why you are making those decisions. So, for example, it is more important to me to save a deposit for a house than to have a new car. You also need to plan shorter-term things, so if you are going on a night out decide in advance how much you are going to spend. I was about to go on TV recently and before we went on air the presenter who was about to interview me said that before the days of contactless payments they would bring a set amount of cash out with them in their pocket on a night out. They would separate their taxi fare into the little pocket in their jeans and when the money they brought was gone and all they were left with was their taxi money, that was the end of their night and they went home. This person was explaining it was simpler for them then. Now they have their card and it is harder for them to decide when a night should end, both from a social and from a financial perspective. Not ignoring the safety concerns of carrying cash, this method is one way we can avoid lots of biases and strangely enough it is something my buddy the TV presenter can self-impose any time they want.

Ultimately a brand might use social triggers to lure you in, but they have hit marketing gold if they can make you feel part of their community. It's inherent in us all to protect and defend our community and we will often go out of pocket and push social boundaries and say things that might annoy others, just to protect what we believe in.

Up the Dubs!

Heuristics and biases summary

Marketing departments and boards of companies are well ahead of us mere mortals when it comes to knowing about and using heuristics and biases to boost their balance sheets. They bring in people who have studied the field and use all the most up-to-date information on the subject to continue to stay ahead.

Don't get me wrong, I don't believe it is a dark art. I am fascinated by the area and I recognise that some of the greatest brains, now and in the past, have studied this field and discovered things about us and our behaviours that are invaluable to us all. These people have entered a cutting-edge field of study that didn't exist 60 or 70 years ago and I would even go as far as to say that I think it is one of the most important fields of study in my world. It is great knowing what we do, but it is even more valuable to know why we do it.

I also admire companies that use these methods to sell more. They should do that. A company's purpose is to make a profit and stay in existence, and any company forward-thinking enough to research and deploy what they have learned in this field has my full admiration. That is, of course, provided that they are using their knowledge for good and not for scamming purposes. Interestingly, the scammers out there utilise our biases probably as well as, if not sometimes better than, the best global firms. We could all learn a lot from them.

Even when it comes to influencers, I am all for them using whatever knowledge they have in order to pursue a successful career and a profitable business for themselves too.

The reason I wanted to include this section of the book is simple. I am all for these companies and individuals using the tools in a fair way to get the most for themselves or their companies. But I want to level the playing field. I have barely scratched the surface here of the biases we all have and how they influence the way we live our lives and spend our money. What I am hoping is that if you haven't noticed them before you start to notice them now and ask yourself whether the decisions you make are truly objective or whether you are being swayed by some clever outside influences. After all, once you start to look for the signs you will start to see loads of red cars on the road.

Planning your financial future

By now I hope you're realising that I don't believe life is about money. I don't even think it is about things. For me life is about experiences and, even more important, experiences with people you love.

Getting on top of and being in control of your money is one of the gateways to having a fulfilled life where you can concentrate your energies on the people in your life who are important to you.

Avoiding some of the common mistakes and recognising that sometimes there are outside influences that nudge you along to make those mistakes, or having you spend money you didn't intend to, is a key part to successfully navigating that life.

But you also need a blueprint, a path that guides you through the steps to take and the pitfalls to avoid when planning your financial future. That's what this section is all about. I'm going to walk through the process I go through when I engage with a new client so that you can see if you need to make any changes for yourself. This is a blueprint, but you do need to recognise its limitations. I have had to use broad brushstrokes because no book will exactly fit you and your specific circumstances. That book – all about you – is what people get when they engage with me or any other decent financial planner and I will not pretend I believe you will get a better outcome by yourself than you would with a decent planner. The stats back me up on that. Let me remind you people who have a good financial planner have 2.5 times the net worth of people who don't when they reach retirement.

The reason I am writing this section and indeed this entire book is because I also believe that there are two types of people who are out there when it comes to personal finances. There are the people who will never engage with a financial planner, and this book is for them, because if they want to do it all by themselves I want to equip them with as many of the tools I possibly can so that they can achieve success. The other type of person is the person who will engage with a planner, and this book is for them too, because I think having this knowledge enables you to engage on a different level with your planner. It will also help you to identify the good ones. Both of which result in better outcomes for all.

So let's jump into the steps I would typically take with a client when we engage.

Establishing where you are

Your net worth

Before you decide where you are going you need to establish where you are. You need to take whatever time it takes to pull all your financial data together. But you also need a quick win. At the outset of this process 'done' is better than 'perfect'. So my recommendation is that you sit down with a pen and paper and split your page into four quadrants, with four different headings.

Then allow yourself 20 minutes to get a rough idea of where you are at. Don't let it run over 20 minutes; this is just your rough guess of where things are at. Once you have everything listed you need to source the supporting documentation. This is where ideally you will transfer this document to an Excel (or other) spreadsheet. If using Excel is just a step beyond your

OWN	OWE
EARN	SPEND

comfort zone, don't worry, you can still do it with pen and paper. You will just lose out on some of the functionality of Excel, but then if you're not a seasoned user of Excel you have no idea what functionality you are missing out on, so does it really matter?

When you go about gathering all your financial docs you can choose to spend days sorting out old drawers full of documents or you can do what a good financial advice firm will do on your behalf, and write to all the main product providers. An email should suffice. There is no problem using general email addresses like info@-type addresses; in fact that can often result in a better outcome because in large firms these addresses are tracked to ensure everything is responded to. A simple email will suffice: give your name and your partner's name, if you have one, your current home address and any previous addresses, your date of birth and your contact details in case they need to ring you. Give details of any policies you know about, but also ask them if they have details of any policies you own that you have not listed. Finally, ask them to send you an up-to-date 'benefit statement'. This will list all the main details you need to start building your financial plan.

When we do this on behalf of a client we contact all the life companies and pension houses, not just the ones our client believes they have business with. You would be surprised how often we find an old SSIA or life assurance policy that the client had forgotten about, so don't assume you don't have some too. Just email them all.

Separately, you may need to email your old employers to track down old pensions. This can be frustrating because you can often be bounced from Billy to Jack between HR, payroll and external pension providers. One thing people often don't realise is that when you write personally to the pension providers they will typically search their retail database for any policies you might have, but it is usually the corporate division that holds any of your old work pensions, particularly if you worked in a big place with loads of staff. So be sure to do both: write directly to the pension provider; and contact your old HR department.

Getting bank, credit union and An Post account balances is a lot more straightforward than trying to root out old pensions. It is often simply a matter of logging into your banking app or walking into a branch, but if for completeness you want to send a letter or email to the institutions, do that too.

You also need to find out the details of any loans you have. To make things simple later in the process, find out how much you owe, how much you pay per month, what the interest rate is and how long is left on the loan.

For most people your income is straightforward – you just grab a recent payslip. I suggest you also get your last payslip from the previous December or, better still, your Employment Details Summary for last year. This is a Revenue document that details how much you were paid and what deductions were applied for last year. If you have more than one income it is much more useful than gathering all your final payslips because it brings them all together on one page. If you are self-employed your Form 11 is the reach-for document, but often a breakdown of your income and deductions from your accountant is the most useful information you need to build your plan.

Ultimately we are gathering details about your income to establish, first, what your gross income is – your income before tax. Then we need to figure out how much in total you paid personally into pensions and, finally, how much your net pay is. This is at the bottom right-hand corner of your payslip and the figure should match the money going into your bank account each week/month.

Finally, you need to establish how much you spend. You can do this in a couple of ways. One is to download your bank statements for the last 12 months and analyse them to establish where your money is going. Interestingly, I have heard of a few people using AI for this. They download their statements, they redact any identifying or personal information and then they upload it to their AI tool of choice. The tool then will tell you where your money is being spent but will also make some suggestions on where to cut back. Some people will be afraid of this and I understand why. But if you are comfortable then it may be a useful exercise, to a point.

These AI tools are most likely the future, but using them does mean that we miss out on an important part of the process. Don't underestimate how powerful it is to do this analysis of your spending yourself. The process and the work it takes often means that you put more value on the results than when it is just handed to you by a bot. This is what's known as the effort justification effect, sometimes called the Ikea effect because people who build their Ikea furniture value that furniture more because they built it than they would have if it were built for them. But it is not just the outcome that's important here. I have seen it with clients for years: they describe how as they go through the figures they slowly start to see the picture emerge of what they are doing right and often what they are doing wrong with the daily spending. It can literally be an awakening. So don't underestimate the process and the value in it.

Having said all that, if you prefer to get it done for you and you're not comfortable uploading it yourself to an AI tool, most banks at this stage have an inbuilt AI tool that will give you a breakdown of your spending. If it is not obvious when you log into your banking app, ask your bank if they do it.

Once you have gathered all your financial information –

what you own, owe, earn and spend – it is time to build on it. Again, you can use pen and paper or a spreadsheet.

You need to build a one-pager that has everything you own and owe. It will be laid out under the following headings. Only record the total values of each item; you don't need to go into how much you pay into them or repayments you make – this will be recorded in your cashflow statement.

- **Non-liquid assets:** These are things like your home, investing property and land. If you own a business the total value of it should be put here too. This is because you can't just shut it down overnight and walk away with whatever it is worth, so therefore it is not liquid.
- **Liquid assets:** This section is split into two parts. The first is cash assets including bank, credit union and An Post. The second is invested assets such as shares, investment portfolio, bonds or funds you hold.
- **Pensions:** Detail all your pensions separately.
- **Loans:** This is just the outstanding balance. Like everything on this sheet, you can list your loans whatever way you want whether that's by the bank you owe the money too or simply 'my car loan', just be sure whatever you call it will make sense to you if you randomly pick this document up again in a year's time.

This document is now your record of truth. Make it clear enough that if the worst came to the worst and your loved ones were trying to figure out where to start looking at your estate they would find it easy to use this document.

The last piece of the puzzle is to add up all the values in each category and then deduct the total value of all your loans to figure out your net worth. Your net worth is the amount of money you would bring with you if you sold everything you owned, cleared your loans and headed to the Caymans or somewhere.

When you are finished it should look something like this:

	JOE	JANE	JOINT & FAMILY	TOTAL
ASSETS				
Non-Liquid				
Home			€400,000	€400,000
Holiday Home			€350,000	€350,000
Total Non-Liquid	€0	€0	€750,000	€750,000
Pensions				
Work Pension	€320,000			€320,000
Total Pension	€320,000	€0	€0	€320,000
Savings				
Current Account		€2,000		€2,000
Credit Union			€10,000	€10,000
Current Account	€2,000			€2,000
Total Savings	€2,000	€2,000	€10,000	€14,000
Investments				
Kids School Fund			€12,300	€12,300
Total Investment	€0	€0	€12,300	€12,300
Total Assets	€322,000	€2,000	€772,300	€1,096,300
LIABILITIES				
Secured				
Mortgage			€280,000	€280,000
Total Secured	€0	€0	€280,000	€280,000
Total Liabilities	€0	€0	€280,000	€280,000
NET WORTH	€322,000	£2,000	€492,300	€816,300

For most people this is often the first time they get to see their net worth all on one page. It can be very empowering to see all you have built. It reflects all the things you have done right and all the things you have done wrong financially in your life, all on one page. Take a minute to take it all in.

Your cashflow

In simple terms, cashflow is simply a record of all the money you have coming in versus all the money you have going out. If you draft up, either on a spreadsheet or a piece of paper, everything coming in and everything going out, you will discover one of two things. Either you have more money coming in than you have going out. This is the best place to be. Or you have more money going out than you have coming in. People often spend years trying to avoid this discovery, but remember, just because you suspected it but didn't check it, it didn't actually make the problem go away. If there was a problem there all along and you ignored it, this is your very first step in solving that problem.

Whether your month is cashflow positive or cashflow negative I would suggest everyone does this. Look at your current account today and figure out how much money you have. Next work out when you are next going to get paid. Then figure out all the things you need to pay for and all the things you want to pay for between now and then. Then give every euro in your bank account a job. You are now the boss of your money. You control it, it does not control you. If you find you don't have enough money to cover everything, you're the boss, you can reallocate the jobs and cover the things you need to first and then the things you want. Doing this exercise regularly means that you will know exactly where you are at any given time in the month and avoid that situation when you end up with too much month left at the end of your money.

You will have identified trends in your spending when you did your analysis earlier, but this process is about seeing the total figures. It is about working out if you are cashflow negative or positive. Where you are negative the process outlined here helps. If you find after cutting back on some things you don't have enough to go around then I would suggest you have some deeper issues and it may be worthwhile asking possibly a trusted friend to have a look at your money with you or going somewhere like MABS.

If you recognise that you have positive cashflow, this is sometimes a red flag. Having positive cashflow and a bank balance that is going up and up over time is okay, but I often come across people who have positive cash flow but little or no savings. This is a result of Parkinson's law – our lifestyle expands to fill the income we have. So if you make more money your lifestyle expands and you spend more money. Positive cashflow with no large accumulation of savings is usually the first sign that you are suffering as a result of Parkinson's law. Identifying this means you can strip out some of the surplus expenditure, which typically does not result in any reduction in the enjoyment of your life, because you are only spending it because you have it.

Doing your cash flow isn't just about trying to identify whether Parkinson's law applies to you: identifying your surplus also gives you something to work with as you build your financial plan. This is important.

It leads to another important point. As you start building your financial plan there will be times when you will have to make guesses. You will have to guess things like what growth you get on your pensions and investments, how much your salary will go up by and also what your future expenditure might be. The important thing to do is first to accept your guess is going to be wrong. Nobody can predict the future, so just accept you are not going to be 100% right. Second, it is really important to guess on the right side of wrong. If I guess a client's investment is going to go up by 4.5% and it goes up by 6%, my financial plan works out. But if I guess it is going to go up by 8% and it achieves 6%, their financial plan blows up and years from now I will be telling a 76-year-old I got it wrong and should never have told them to retire.

When it comes to your expenses, if you're not sure, guess up. So if you don't know how much your grocery shopping is, make an estimate and add a bit extra. This does two things: it means you will have guessed on the right side of wrong and, more important, it allows you to have confidence in your financial plan. When I present a client with their financial plan they will often ask, 'But does this include X expense or Y expense? What about inflation? Have you allowed for that?' It is only when they realise I have that they really start to believe in the plan.

You need to remember at this point that you need to have confidence in each building block you add to your plan. If you cut corners or don't include something, when it all comes together you will be worried about the foundations of your plan and you won't have full confidence in it.

Where are you going?

Now you have established where you are, you need to decide where you are trying to get to. You need to revisit some of the conversations we discussed at the very start of the book about the things you want to achieve, the places you want to go and the experiences you want to have.

These need to be plotted out. Pen and paper is fine. For example, if you want to go on a safari, try to figure out how much it will cost and when you want it to happen. If it is going to cost €12,000 and you want to do it in ten years' time, you need to allow for this in your plan by putting aside €1,200 per annum, which is €100 per month. Sometimes this can be daunting but, remember, unless you're flush with cash you are not going to wake up in 12 years' time and €12,000 will have magically appeared from somewhere to enable you to go. But doing this calculation also has another impact; it makes you bring it into today. You might think 'I want to go on a safari someday' and you might really truly want to. Saying 'someday' makes it a 'future you' problem, but deciding that you have to start saving for it today, you have to make some sacrifices today, makes it a 'today you' problem and often helps you focus on whether or not you really want to do it. Some people will have the attitude that 'I will go on safari in 12 years' time *if* the business sells that year/*if* I inherit that money/*if* my investment fund does well …' and that's different. That's an 'I will *if*' goal and is not really dependent on sacrifices today.

It is important to name your goals and map them out, but it's equally important to name your savings accounts. If, for example, you have a savings account called Rainy Day Fund and you go through a rough patch or a tough day or you simply have an urge to splurge some cash, it is quite easy to say, 'I'll take it from my Rainy Day Fund, sure it's raining now.' But if you call your savings account by the name of its purpose – Siobhán's College Fund or Safari Fund – that emotional attachment helps you think straight when you go to raid it.

When you have all your goals costed and on a timeline you can see if they are affordable or if you need to adjust some things. For example, some people won't be able to afford €100 per month but would be willing to set aside €1,200 once a year from their bonus, and that's okay. (We'll talk about where this money goes when we talk about the five-year rule.)

Work out your goals but for now don't include your pension calculations; they are more straightforward than you might think, and we'll tackle that later.

Your buffer

Some people call this a rainy day or emergency fund. I don't like these terms because for me they conjure up negative connotations. A buffer is used when life happens and that might be life good or life bad! So for example the boiler blows up and needs to be replaced or you get an invoice to a wedding (sorry, I meant invite …).

People without a buffer reach for the credit card when these financial 'surprises' happen. I say 'surprises' because people who implement the buffer properly find after a full year that the things we called financial surprises in the past are no longer surprises. There are actually very few true financial surprises, there are just things that happen that we weren't prepared for, so we call them surprises to make ourselves feel better about it. Christmas happens every year. So does a holiday, for most people, as does going back to school. Waking up in January with a financial hangover and telling yourself you were surprised by how much Christmas cost is just a way of letting yourself feel okay about it. I don't want to be harsh about this – there are things that can take us by surprise financially – but using a buffer properly totally diminishes these occurrences.

You should have between three and six months' take-home pay in your buffer. If you have a joint-income household where the income is very consistent, three months is enough, but if for example you are a single-income household and your pay is erratic – perhaps you get a large lump sum when you complete a project and then nothing for a few months, which is often the case for certain tradespeople or freelancers – you need six months' worth. You will know your own setup, so you can decide what is most appropriate for you.

Don't think I don't recognise the significance of the amounts of money I am talking about here. They are significant and it does take time to build them up, but it is important. Your buffer is your financial security blanket. The difference between having a buffer and not having one is the difference between being able to turn over and fall back to sleep at 3 a.m. versus having yet another sleepless night worrying about money.

Having said that it is daunting, there is also good news. Research has shown that having $500 as a buffer (it was US research) dramatically reduces our level of financially anxiety. So if you have no buffer, over the next few weeks and months start to build towards getting to the €500 mark so you can start to feel the benefit of this. It's okay if, as life happens, you dip into your buffer as you build it – that's what it's for. But you do need to try to put a regular amount aside each month to try to build it over time.

When you use the buffer, two things should happen next. First, the same way you would if you had put the expense on the credit card, you have to try to replace the money you took from the buffer as soon as possible. You need to treat your buffer like a separate entity from yourself – this will make you respect it more, but we are also much better at looking after other people's money and things than we are our own. (We'll see that in action later, when we discuss prescriptions for ourselves versus those for a pet.)

The second thing is where the real magic comes in. When you have to dip into the buffer you need to learn from what just happened. Let's say the tyres go on your car and you need to replace them. You don't have the money in cashflow this month so you reach for the buffer. Let's assume the four tyres cost €600 to replace. Then you remember that you had to replace all those tyres this time last year. So now you put €50 a month aside so that this time next year you will have €600 to put towards the tyres. If you absolutely can't afford the €50, make it €25 or €10 or whatever you can. Putting anything aside is better than putting nothing aside and it will leave you in a better position next year. Where you put the money is up to you: you could have a physical envelope marked Tyres or it could be a pocket, space or wallet on your fintech bank app. It does, however, need to be named so that you create that emotional attachment to the money and in future if you are tempted to dip into it you know exactly what you are taking from. You do not save it in your buffer – that's separate.

After 12 months of operating this system you will start to find financial surprises start to disappear. I am not saying they don't happen, but they will no longer be surprises because you will be prepared for them.

This system is something that traditionally I only spoke to certain clients about. But now I suggest it to all my clients, whatever their wealth. This system identifies why people often end up being short at the end of the month, it answers the question 'I earn good money but where does it all go?' and it doesn't take account of wealth. Some people never adopt it, and that's okay. But the ones who do find it a game-changer.

Short-term goals

Once you have started to build your buffer you need to look at what you need to plan for in the short term. Start with things you expect to happen over the next 12 months. If you go on holiday every July, work out how many months away it is, how much you will need for it and then divide one by the other to figure out how much you need to set aside per month. Do the same for other things like car and home insurance, back to school, dentist's appointments, etc. Try to draw up a robust list of all the things you expect to happen and start planning for them in exactly the same way you do when you had a buffer expense.

Be sure to name all the envelopes, pocket spaces or wallets you decide to use. By doing this you are taking full control. You are the boss now. You control your money; it does not control you. Imagine this scenario: you have ten different envelopes, marked with July Holiday, Back to School, Dentist and so on. And life happens and you need money. The amount you need is more than your buffer. You look at all the envelopes and you start to move the money around. Remember, you are the boss. You decide what jobs your money is going to do. You can decide to change the jobs as life changes.

Medium-term goals

Next map out your goals for the medium term, typically a one-year to ten-plus-year time horizon. Go through the same process as before: work out what the goal is; name the account; decide when will it be; and set aside money between now and then to meet the goal.

It is important at this point to accept that when you map out your buffer, short-term and medium-term goals you may find it quite overwhelming and even a little daunting. You may also realise you just don't have enough money to cover everything you want to do. Although it may not feel like it, this is a good thing. We all have hopes and dreams and we expect that someday we will achieve them. Then we wake up and we are 90 years old and we didn't get to them. When we map out the things we want to achieve and realise some things are beyond our reach we have choices. We can remove some of them. We can change the goal. We might try and find ways to increase our income. Or maybe we can decide to cut our expenditure in other areas. We can prioritise our goals in a different way.

Can you see what happens in this moment, though? You get to make decisions. You recognise the problems in advance. These problems were always there, you were just either unaware of them or ignoring them But you also realise that because you have identified them in advance you now have options. Possibly for the first time ever, you are the boss. You control your money, it does not control you.

Tackling debt

There are two types of debt – happy debt and crappy debt. Happy debt is typically a loan that is hard to get, is often cheaper and is used to buy things that go up in value over long periods of time, like property, so we are talking about a mortgage.

Crappy debt is easier to get, is typically expensive and is used to buy things that go down in value, like a car, or is consumed straightaway, like a meal in a restaurant. For example, loans like buy now pay later, credit cards, personal loans, car loans or overdrafts.

If you just have a mortgage you can still get ahead financially. But if you are carrying a lot of crappy debt you are on a financial treadmill and you are going to find it very difficult to get ahead. You will be stuck in a financial loop. Once you have made a start building a decent buffer you must tackle your crappy debt as an absolute priority.

If you have some savings, provided you don't clear yourself out completely, I would strongly suggest using some of this savings to reduce the debt. I know it feels hard to let go of the savings, but if you don't you are literally stuck in a rut.

I could write an entire book on debt, but for the purposes of this book just know that crappy debt is bad and you need to address it. You won't get ahead financially if you don't.

The secret savings plan only one in three people use

There is a savings plan available to you and you probably don't even use it. But I can promise you most of the really rich are on to it. I want you to consider how this works and then decide if I were to sit down with you would you be willing to do it or not?

You will sit with me and I will fill out some paperwork. Each month, or once a year if you would prefer, you will transfer some of your money to an account in the Cayman Islands. The great thing is I can sort it for you that you take the money that's going into this scheme from your wages before you get taxed. In other words you can save using your before-tax income instead of your after-tax income.

Once it lands in the Cayman Islands I can have it invested for you. We can buy safe funds that have you investing in all the biggest companies in the world and we will even lend some of your money to governments. The best bit is when it grows; because it is in the Caymans, you won't pay any tax on the growth.

Years from now I will organise to have some of the money brought back to Ireland for you in one go and I will get that bit back into Ireland without you having to pay any tax. The rest of it we will bring back as and when you need it, but when we bring it back you will have to pay income tax on it.

Would you do it?

What if I told you that once it is set up I can get a letter from Revenue telling you that they know all about it and they approve of the scheme.

Would you do it then?

Obviously I am not a dodgy salesperson and obviously this all sounds a bit suspect, but it actually isn't. Read through the story again but replace 'Cayman Islands' with the word 'pension'.

Basically you save into a pension using your before-tax income, not your after-tax income. You can invest it and when it grows you don't pay tax on the growth. When you retire you get some of it tax-free and you pay tax on the balance.

People get hung up on what pensions are, but they are simply savings plans with brilliant tax incentives. Our pension rules are the envy of many other jurisdictions. Yet there is huge swathes of people in Ireland who ignore them.

I will say this very clearly: for an employee there is no better way to save in Ireland than a pension.

You will notice that I didn't include a long-term section here; that's because a pension is what you need for long-term investing in Ireland. Depending on your age you can invest 15–40% of your salary into a pension and if you can afford to do that but you are not, that is financial insanity.

If you are in a work scheme and you are getting matching contributions from your employer you need to take full advantage of that too. I have come across people who tell me if they put in 4% their boss puts in 4% and I say, 'So are you doing the four per cent?', to which they reply, 'Nah, I'm only doing two per cent, but they match that with two per cent, so it's okay.'

No, it's not okay, not at all. If you can afford it and you

are not maxing what you can get from your boss in the work pension scheme you are basically telling your boss 'You know that pay rise you offered me? I don't want it, thanks.'

Equally, if you can afford to go to the max that Revenue will allow and you are not doing it you are basically telling Revenue that you want to pay more tax than you need to. When you put money into your pension you pay less tax. That's how it works.

Let me give you a simple example of the power of employers' contributions and tax relief versus saving outside a pension. I'll use a higher-rate taxpayer for the purpose of the example.

When you pay €100 into a pension you pay €40 less in tax. In other words, it costs you €60 to put €100 in. Looking at the same thing in a slightly different way, if your take-home pay is €1,000 per month and you put €100 into your pension your take-home pay would only reduce by €60, so it would go down from €1,000 to €940. So it cost you €60 to get €100 into your pension. You can use €100 of your before-tax salary and your take-home pay will only reduce by €60.

The maths is the same with bigger numbers: €100 costs €60, €1,000 costs €600 and so on. The maths on an employer matching contribution are even more straightforward. You put in €1 (which actually only costs you €0.60) and they put in €1. You put in €2 and they put in €2 and so on.

Let's imagine somebody want to use €100 of their salary to save for their future. To try level the playing field somewhat and more importantly to simplify things lets ignore USC and PRSI but we will include income tax.

If Salt uses €100 per month of their salary, as a higher rate tax payer they pay €40 in income tax they are left with €60 to save long term. For the 40 years of their career they invest exactly €60 per month in a fund that achieves 6% growth per annum and after allowing for tax on the growth they end up with a fund of just under €68,000.

But Pepper sees that when they save in their pension, they can use their before tax income instead of the after tax income. So Pepper gets to save the full €100 of their salary. Pepper also gets a matching employer contribution of €100 because that's how their works scheme is set up. By the end of the 40 years of contributions Pepper ends up with a pension pot of just over €446,500.

Remember the net cost for Salt and Pepper was exactly the same, it was €60 per month. It was the same money being used in a different way getting a much better result.

I can't stress enough how good our pension system is, and if you are not taking advantage of it you need to because I can promise you others are.

Putting your surplus income to work

Once you have sorted your buffer and your short-term, medium-term and long-term goals you need to see if you have any money left from your monthly cashflow. It sounds like a big expectation, so don't be worried if you have nothing spare from your month to month. Look at all you have achieved; it's phenomenal. But if when you look at your total income and compare it to your total outgoings, including contributions to your goals, and you do have anything to spare you need to put that money to good use and invest it.

It is really important to put a plan around having that money whipped out of your monthly cash and put elsewhere, otherwise Parkinson's law will kick in.

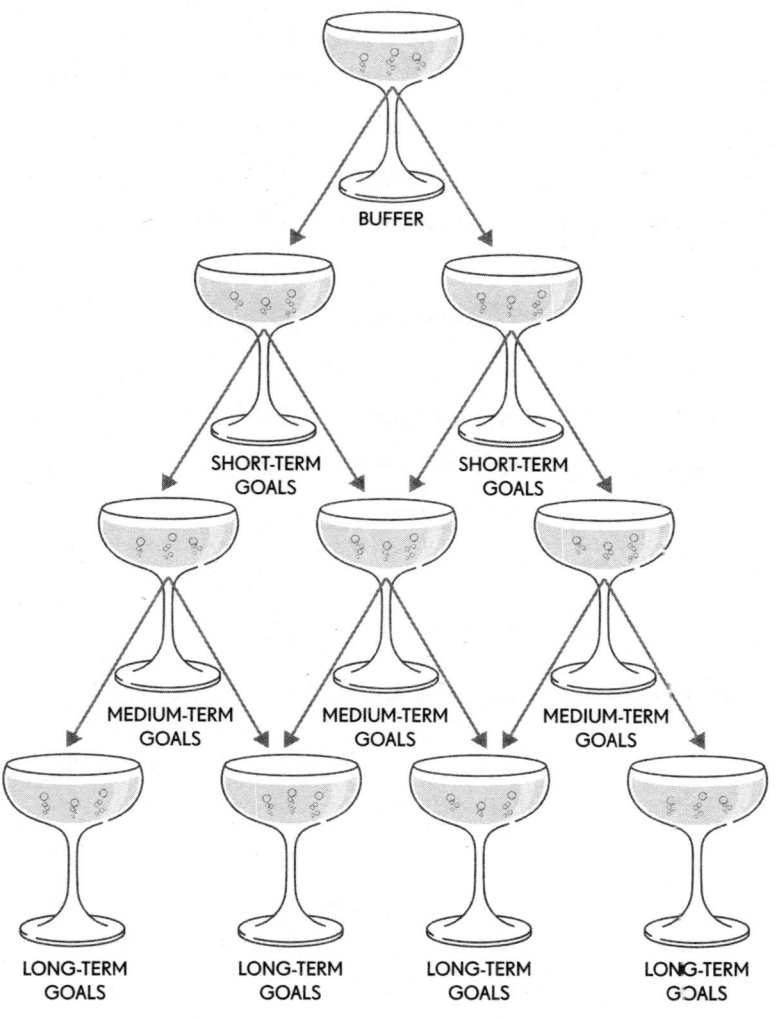

Equally, you need to look at your accounts, including bank, credit union and/or An Post and decide to apportion any money you have there. Start by allocating to your goals in the order buffer, short-term, medium-term and long-term. If there is any spare beyond that, you need to get it working harder by investing it.

Imagine your entire finances are like a champagne tower. As the money comes in at the top it goes into the first glass, your buffer. When that fills it overflows into your short-term goals. The next layer is medium-term goals, and finally there are your long-term retirement goals. Once all these glasses are full you have likely reached financial independence and then you can start considering adding a new layer, which is passing on your wealth to the next generation. But equally, if you don't establish the structure at the start, the money comes in at the top and then just spills everywhere, never to be seen again, and leaving you wondering where it has gone.

Investing your money

Once you have identified any spare cash or lump sums that are ready to be put to good use you then have to invest, as long as you follow the five-year rule (which I'll explain later).

I'm not going to go into a lot of detail about how to invest money here – that's been addressed in my previous books. Instead, I'm going to talk about what you shouldn't do. These are investment mistakes I see all the time.

Investing mistakes

1. Not investing at all

We have considered this earlier, but let's remind ourselves. If you put €10,000 on deposit for 5 years at 0.5%, ignoring tax and using simple interest it will mature at €10,250. But something that costs €10,000 today, allowing for 2% inflation and using simple interest again, will cost €11,000 in five years' time. If you think this is bad over five years using simple interest it is much worse over 20, 30, 40 or even 50 years using compound interest.

In fact, using the same maths, again ignoring tax but compounding it and looking at it over 30 years, the bank deposit will go from €10,000 to €11,614 and the thing you want to buy will go from €10,000 to €18,113, which means that over that period you will have lost €6,499 of your purchasing power. That's serious damage.

Investing can be risky and scary and people often don't do it because they are worried about losing money. Yes, investments do go up and down, but they do that on an upward trend. But if you leave your money in a bank account you are guaranteed to lose money to inflation over a long time period. So you can go up and down on an upward long-term trend or you can choose to lose money. You decide.

2. Timing the market

It's 'time in' the market, not 'timing'. I often have this conversation with new clients. They get to the end of the financial planning process and we are going through the things that need to be implemented and what products we need to help them buy. They have given me feedback that they have got a huge amount from the process and often describe how for the first time ever they have real clarity on their long-term financial future. They recognise that they need to change some things to achieve the goals we have laid out because, as

I always say, a plan is just words on a piece of paper. The plan doesn't change anything, but you can change things based on what the plan suggests.

Then the client says, 'Yeah, we'll do it all, but we would prefer to wait a while, just because, you know, the world is very unsettled at the moment and it just doesn't seem a good time to invest.'

They're right – the world is very unsettled right now and it doesn't even matter when 'now' is. Think back over the last 20, 30 or even 50 years – can you tell me any year when the world was calm, without any worries, no uncertainties and settled? The fact is, the world is always unsettled, there is no time where we all sit back and say, 'The world, 'tis grand at the minute, isn't it?'

Then they say 'Yes, but this time is different,' and I have to say I agree. The circumstances are often different, but what we must remember is the outcomes are often the same.

As we discussed in the introduction to this book, we have a major market event every three to five years, and 80% of stock market crashes fully recover within three years. So if you are really unlucky, and you get the timing all wrong, wait three years and the probability is that it will all be okay again. You should be applying the five-year rule anyway (covered later), so what difference does it make?

People try to avoid the bad days but by doing so they miss the good ones. Put in your money when you have it, take it out when you need it and leave a long time in between. The rest is just noise.

3. Overreacting to ups and downs

Early in 2025 we had a big decline in markets. It was at the start of Donald Trump's second administration and stock markets around the world were reacting to some of the changes that were being announced. It was a turbulent time.

We spend a lot of time during our financial planning process preparing clients for turbulence like this. So I was really interested to see how clients would react. This isn't scientific, but I did clock it mentally as it happened. I wanted to gauge how many clients contacted us to say they were scared and wanted their money out versus how many rang and said 'You told me markets go down from time to time, I have some cash and I want to put it in.'

When you truly understand markets you accept that they will go down, but you trust the research and therefore you know they will recover – and then you can take advantage of it. The rich aren't running away from markets when they fall apart. When everyone else is running away they are running towards them because they recognise that this is when the bargains are available.

In no other area of our lives would we react to a discount the way we do with investing. Whether it's a car, a house or a pair of jeans, if we see them on sale we are more compelled to buy them. If we weren't no company would ever do a sale again.

A stock market crash is simply a big sale. The best companies in the world have just dropped in value. They are still the same companies as they were yesterday, they are just cheaper. They are on sale. So why do we run away?

Missing the downs would be great, but history shows us that the best days come immediately after the worst ones. It would be amazing if a bell rang at the bottom to tell us all that this is it, it's all up from here. But a bell doesn't ring so we have to stay invested if we want to capture the best days.

Missing the best days can be expensive. Let's say you put €1,000 into the world stock markets for ten years in 2015. If you just left it alone, on 31 December 2024, ignoring tax, it would have grown to €3,016. But let's say you got spooked at the start of Covid. You believed this time was different; after all, it was a global pandemic. Everything was shut down. Things were never going to be the same again. You took your money out and sat on the sidelines waiting for things to calm down. You waited. You waited a bit longer. All the while markets were going up. You waited a full six months and eventually put your money back in on 15 September 2020, when you had been out of the market for a full six months. They just happened to be the best six months in the ten years you were invested for and you missed them. Instead of your €1,000 turning into €3,016, because you missed just six months out of the 120 months you were invested for your return is reduced by almost a third. You would have €2,191 instead of €3,016.

You might think 'But I wouldn't stay out for six months; I'd go back in when I saw it going back up again', but even if you only missed the best week, which in that ten-year period was the week ending 8 April 2020, your return would have dropped from €3,016 down to €2,645.

MISSING THE BEST CONSECUTIVE DAYS
MSCI World Index Total Return 2015-2024

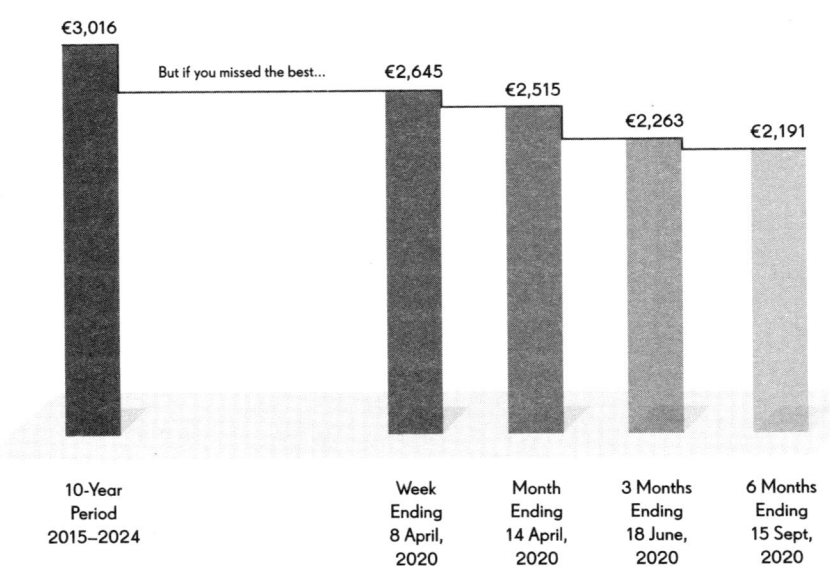

Past performance does not predict future returns.

On the other hand, when things are going really well, people often take the attitude that 'When shares are at an all-time high there's only one way to go from here.' That isn't true. Remember when I said that shares go up and down but on an upward trend? It is the upward trend bit that is important; because they are on an upward trend they will always be hitting all-time highs.

I was in California this year and I met a guy on the beach early one morning. He was in his mid- to late 70s and taking his daily early-morning walk. He wore a T-shirt that read 'I plan to live forever. So far so good.' His attitude was infectious, and he seemed to really love life. His T-shirt resonated with me because I realised that he must have had good days and bad days in his life. Just like shares, he has had his ups and downs, but, like shares, he is on an upward trend. The day I met him was at an all-time high for the number of days he had been alive. It's the same for you: today you hit an all-time high in how old you are.

When things move on an upward trend it won't always be a straight line, it will waver, but it is the start and the end points that matter. If the stock market isn't hitting all-time highs over long periods of time then it is going backwards, so I do find the scary headline 'Shares at an all-time high' somewhat nonsensical.

But the maths backs me up, between 1970 and 2024 there were a total of 660 months. Of those 660 months, 139 ended with an 'all-time high'. That means 139 times in 660 months, or 21% of the time, a newspaper editor could plaster across the front page 'Shares hit all-time high' and be 100% correct. But to use this piece of data to suggest that things are going to fall off a cliff is a stretch. In fact, on average, one year after an all-time high the global market is up 8.3%; three years later it is up 8.5%; and six years later it is, on average, up 7.7%. Compare that to any one-, three- or five-year period and the average returns are not wildly different; they are 9.6%, 8.2% and 8.2% respectively.

If we assess the returns immediately after an all-time high and compare them to the average returns over the entire period they are very similar. So what use is a headline telling us that shares are at an all-time high? Of course they are – that's what they do. The only shares that get a boost from that headline is the shares of the newspaper because scary headlines sell newspapers.

My advice? Ignore the headlines and remember it is time in the markets – not timing the markets – that's important.

4. Chasing the next big thing

The next big thing might be crypto, gold, NFTs or some other thingy we haven't seen or heard of yet. Statistically you have to invest in 22 next big things for one to work out. The reality is that the people who make money on the next big thing have either forgotten or are failing to tell you about the money they lost on the first 21. Or else they landed on 22 by pure chance. I know people will say 'It was different for me; I did my research and saw the opportunity and I took it', and guess what? It makes absolutely no difference if I believe you or not; the important thing is that you believe you.

When we were filming *How to be Good with Money* a few years back, there was a rush on crypto. It was doing exceptionally well. Lots of people were going in for the first time. When the contributors started handing over their bank statements for me to assess for the show about half of them had bought some crypto. The hype was high!

We had a production meeting and it was agreed that we would bring crypto into the show and discuss it in detail as an informative piece. However, in the weeks between getting their documents and the filming actually taking place crypto crashed and lots of people lost money. When we started filming we pressed ahead with the plan to explore crypto. But every single person had not only sold out, they had all lost money and were never going near it again. We had no story to tell, so we dropped it.

What had happened to these people was exactly what can go wrong when somebody ventures into what they see as 'investing'; they get burned and potentially they are scarred for life and never want to go back into investing again. Destined for a life of money sitting in bank accounts losing against inflation.

Every generation has one of these types of events, and the last generational event in Ireland was probably Eircom shares. If you are lucky enough to be too young to remember what happened with Eircom, let me explain. The state owned it and decided to sell it. As a nation we were encouraged to buy shares in it when it floated on the stock market. It didn't go very well and people lost money. To this day people come into my office and say 'I don't like shares. Remember Eircom?'

When you get burned, particularly early in your life, you tread much more carefully in the future. It can often do irreparable damage. Equally, if things go right with a next big thing you don a Superman cape and think people like me are boring and that we just don't get it.

Let me say this very clearly: people make lots of money on things like crypto and other next big things. I am not saying you can't; I am simply saying the odds are so badly stacked against you that it is not a risk I am willing to take with either my money or my clients' money.

Some people are always going to chase the next big thing. If they hit the bullseye they can be rewarded handsomely and get rich quick. For me, I am happy to get rich slow.

5. Not understanding the power of compounding

Compounding is getting interest on interest, and it is powerful. In some of my calculations in this book I mention simple interest. This is something I use a lot because it is easy maths. If I'm on the radio or TV and I'm asked a question I can do the simple interest calculations in my head, but if I were to do the compounding calculation I would need to whip out my calculator, and not just any auld ordinary calculator but my HP 10BII fancy financial calculator. (If you really want to nerd out and do things that excite us financial planners, get yourself one of these and use YouTube to teach yourself how to use it. I have a physical one but I also have a deadly app I use on my phone which looks and works exactly the same as the physical one.)

If you have €10,000 invested and are getting 10% growth per annum, this will grow to €20,000 over ten years using simple interest. It's simple: 10% of €10,000 is €1,000, so multiply that by ten and you get €10,000 in interest over ten years.

But €10,000 over ten years of 10% compound interest turns into €25,937. (Yes, I had to use my special calculator for that one.)

I don't want to teach you how suck eggs, but let's make sure there is no confusion here. Simple interest is a straightforward calculation where we add the 10% per year but we work out the 10% based on the original investment amount. Compound interest is calculated using the end-of-year balance.

At the end of year one in our example both accounts get €1,000 in interest. It's easy: 10% of €10,000 is €1,000. When it comes to the second year calculation, with simple interest you go back to the start and work out 10% of the original €10,000, which is €1,000 again. But with compounding you work out 10% of the new balance, which is now €11,000. So in year two you get €1,100 in interest and each year this compounding gets bigger.

You are now either screaming at the page that this is bloody obvious or you are wondering what the hell I'm talking about. If you are the latter just know that compounding is better and it is very powerful over time.

Your €10,000 invested today will be worth €108,000 in 25 years' time. So it takes 25 years for it to go up 11-fold. But ten years later, after 35 years, it will be worth €281,000. It took 25 years to get 11 times bigger but then give it another ten years and will be 28 times bigger. After 45 years it will be worth €728,000.

To think about compounding in a different way altogether, imagine it is snowing. You have a snowball in your hand and you put it on the ground and start to roll it. At the start it gets a bit bigger, but soon snow packs on snow (interest on interest) and it is gathering momentum. The first few rolls gather a bit but once you get going it gets bigger at an exponential rate. Soon the snowball is so big that every push is gathering massive amounts of snow and that snow is gathering more snow and the cycle continues.

But what use to you is knowing how compounding works? It is a reminder that the sooner you start, the better. It is never too early to start investing, but it is also never too late. The rich know all about compounding, and they know compounding is the reason the rich keep getting richer.

6. Overconfidence

Have you heard of the Dunning-Kruger effect? In simple terms, it means that people with little or no competence on a subject can speak with great authority on it. It is not because they are trying to trick you into believing them, it is because they actually believe themselves.

A little bit of knowledge is dangerous. You just don't know what you don't know and this can result in over-confidence.

Take investing, for example. Somebody with very little knowledge could confidently say 'This investment does 12% per annum' and they might be so sure of themselves that you take them at their word. Yet a seasoned financial adviser might look at the exact same investment opportunity and say 'This has done 12% in a year, once before. It might do it again or it might do more or less than that. It might even lose money some years.'

Sometimes people are out-and-out scammers and they are telling lies. But more often than not the person making a claim just does not know what they don't know and their only fault is over-confidence. But sometimes I am faced with somebody who believes they know more about investing than not just me but also the academics I rely on for research to help guide how to invest clients' money.

Everyone is entitled to their own opinion, but nobody is entitled to their own facts. I love a robust discussion. I love it when a client really challenges me on how and why I think investments work in a certain way. For me that is where the real learning is, but it is also an opportunity for me to truly understand how my client is thinking.

I have been lucky enough in my career to have been in the presence of Eugene Fama and Robert Merton. I'd be surprised if you know who they are, but in my world they are a big deal. They have both been awarded the Nobel Prize for their work in economics. You would think that they know everything there is to know on their subject matter. But what I found amazing watching them both in a room full of a few hundred people was how humble they were. Not only, as you might expect, did they have respect for each other's opinion, they also had a true interest in and respect for anything being said from the audience. It dawned on me as I watched them interact that these guys are listening with genuine intent and respect for what was being said. Then I realised they are still learning, seeking the opportunity to learn in every interaction.

I think that's where the less competent and often slightly cocky individual falls down. They have led themselves into a false belief that they know everything there is to know and therefore don't need to learn. So a word of warning: don't mistake confidence for competence and always be open to learning.

7. Reading the papers

There are a lot of things going on outside your front door. We have economic failures and successes. We have horrendous conflicts and we have humanitarian situations that would literally bring you to the depths of despair. All of these things are important. But more often than not, whether global events are positive or negative there is little or nothing you as an individual can do about them. Even the most powerful politicians, central bankers, economists or business people around the world cannot influence change alone. Collectively, though, we can influence change. We have a voice and we can make it heard through our political representation and other channels, I am not discounting that. I am certainly not telling you to ignore what happens around the world. What I am suggesting, however, is that as a long-term investor, as somebody who controls their own money, be careful with how much space this stuff rents in your head; and be acutely alert not to allow the daily noise affect your long-term thinking.

As you go through an ordinary day you will come in contact with people. Every single one of those people has an agenda. The agenda might be very obvious – they want to sell you something. Or they might be driven by something important to them and they want to change your opinion. Or maybe they have some good news and want to share it with you. It could be as simple as wanting human interaction, and you might be the only opportunity they have for that today.

Whatever the reason, good or bad, we do need to recognise

that every human interaction, however simple or complex, is driven by some motivation on both sides. For you, your motivation might be to talk your way out of the conversation as soon as possible! But it is still a motivation.

We also need to consider these motivations when it comes to the content we are served up online and through the media. The media, both social and traditional, is typically trying to sell you something or at the very least hold your attention long enough to sell advertising to people who want to get ads in front of you.

Research suggests that when we have a good experience in a restaurant we tell up to five people; when we have a bad one we tell upwards of ten people. This can be explained somewhat by negativity bias, where the pain of a negative is greater than the joy from an equal positive. This greater intensity brings with it stronger feelings, such as irritation, frustration or even anger, and when we have intense feelings about things we tend to react. One way we can react is by talking about the experience to others.

If we accept this to be true then you can see why bad news travels fast. So if you were the editor of a media outlet, would you go with the positive headline or the negative one?

Long-term investors are in it for the long run. When you think about yesterday's news you can probably remember several of the headlines. But if I ask you to remember what happened 11 years ago, or 17 years ago, or any year in the distant past I bet you will remember at best one global economic event that happened in or around that year. Guess what? Markets' memory is exactly the same. When you look at the line on the graph that shows the historical returns of a stock market, if the timeline is long enough, events that were major at the time appear as a blip or maybe a dent on a line that is moving upwards from left to right. Markets only remember the big stuff, but the media serves you a fresh helping every day of the noise that ultimately will likely not even show up as a blip for the long-term investor.

I think we should all read the news and be aware and care about what's going on around the world but we also need to recognise the noise of today is not the long-term investor's friend.

8. Not diversifying

I was having a chat with a new client yesterday who has done incredibly well with a tiny selection of shares. He owns shares in Netflix and Amazon and a few others. In total he owns shares in fewer than five companies. He has had exceptional return. I won't put his numbers here, but I will give you the maths. It works out that for every €100,000 he invested he is now holding €1.6 million. In other words he turned every €100,000 into €1.6 million.

Guess what he is going to do next? Exactly what I have asked him to do: he is going to cash them in and move them to a well-constructed, well-diversified portfolio. There are several reasons I am asking him to do this.

First, because of his success he has now reached financial independence, so by staying invested in this small selection of shares he is taking unnecessary risk. He literally does not need the return, so he does not need to take the risk associated with holding such a concentrated portfolio.

I have been very clear that I am not recommending he move from his basket of shares to my well-constructed, well-diversified portfolio in the expectation or hope that my investment is going to perform better. I am doing it to dilute the risk. For me, holding shares in fewer than five companies is closer to betting than investing.

The other thing I can guarantee him is that if he moves to the broader portfolio he will definitely own the best-performing companies on the stock market next year. He will also own the worst and everything in between, because I buy the entire market. The good, the bad and the stuff in the middle. This means that, provided the good performers cover the losses of the worst performers, he will get the return of the shares in the middle.

These reasons are exactly the same reasons that I ask clients who hold shares in the company they work for to do the same. But there is an added complication if you have built a significant portion of wealth from the shares you have accumulated from your employer's share option scheme or free shares you have been given. I don't like people having their wealth and their income tied to the same individual company and I don't care which company that is or what their track record or future expectations are. My advice is the same: take part in any scheme you are offered to the maximum you can afford and when the shares vest, do not spend the money but move it to a well-constructed, well-diversified portfolio. Yes, you might miss out on some growth and yes, it might be exceptional; but we have all heard of (and I have had to pick up the pieces for) people who have suffered the nightmare of layoffs in work and a share price that has tanked. Diversification is your friend here. Use it.

Diversification doesn't just give you exposure to the best- and worst-performing shares; done right it also spreads your money across every country in the world and every sector. This means you don't miss out on a particular region, like emerging markets, having a good year and you don't have to guess what sector is going to have a really great run.

Diversification is not just a pretty pie chart; it is a clever way of being sure you are part of the next big thing.

9. Thinking short term – future aversion

Consider this first-world problem for a minute. Go with your initial gut feeling and be honest!

Would you rather €1 million today, or would you prefer to get one cent today that doubles every day for 30 days? In other words, you get €0.01 today, then tomorrow you get €0.02 and the day after you get €0.04. As I typed this I jumped on Instagram and asked my followers. Roughly 50% of over 10,000 people voted for the €1 million up front. But when you do the maths, the cent doubling each day over 30 days actually amounts to €10.7 million! Did that make you change your mind?

What's at play here is future aversion or, put more simply, short-term thinking. We value things today more than we do things in the future. This is something you need to be very mindful of when it comes to your long-term financial future. We may struggle to put money away today because it will be ages before we get it back. We may be impatient when it comes to allowing the compounding effect to kick in. But we may also overlook the value of long-term investing in favour of enjoying today.

10. Being emotional

There are lots of places where money and emotion cross. Sometimes it is extremely useful, like when we name our savings and create an emotional attachment. But at other times it can be damaging because we make decisions with our heart instead of our head.

Remember, financial planning is just a process. It is a means to have our money support the life we want to have. Money itself has zero emotion, but money can bring us lots of emotions, both happy and sad.

Every time you make a financial decision you need to ask yourself two questions:

1. Is this an emotional or a rational decision I am making?
2. Could this decision be improved by adding emotion to it or subtracting emotion from it?

Emotion can be our friend or our foe. Recognise the difference and you can master it.

Summary

I hope having read this far you are coming to the conclusion that markets go up and down but are on an upward trend, that trying to time when to get in or out is a futile exercise and that the media is not a friend of the long-term investor. We could try chasing the next big thing or we could use diversification to guarantee we are part of the next big thing.

But more than anything else I hope you get the feeling that investing done right is boring and it is simple. I believe it is made overly complex to create jobs for the boys (and girls).

Be happy to get rich slow. If you do, you won't get poor fast.

Your master plan

When you have allocated your money to your short-, medium- and long-term goals, you need to apply the five-year rule and be aware of Parkinson's law.

The five-year rule

This is a must when it comes to your financial plan. The five-year rule is simple: you need to look at your bank, credit union or An Post account regularly and ask yourself 'Do I have money here that I do not need in the next five years?' If the answer is yes, you need to take it out of there and get it working for you. Invest it.

The same applies to your income. If you have surplus income that you won't need in the next five years, you need to get it invested. If you might need the money in the next five years, you leave in a deposit account and put up with the awful interest rates. And you lose money against inflation.

This also applies to any lump sums you might get in the future. Clients often ask, 'What do I do with the lump sum that I get from my pension? Do I just leave it in the bank and spend it?' The answer is that you apply the five-year rule.

When you have a financial planner they will at the very least at every review hold you to task and review your finances and flag it if you are carrying too much cash. But if you are doing it all yourself you need to do it regularly. I suggest it should be part of your routine; once a quarter, every six months or at the very least once a year, check your balances and make the call on whether there is any money that is surplus to requirements.

Parkinson's law

As we've seen, Parkinson's law is the rule that says a job will take as long as the time you have available. The task expands to fill the time you have. In my experience, about 85% of my clients suffer a similar fate when it comes to money. If you make €50,000 a year you spend €50,000. But if you make €60,000 you spend €60,000, lifestyle creep kicks in and your spending habits adjust to fill the income you have.

When it comes to financial planning, once you have all your money allocated to your short-, medium- and long-term goals and you have allocated any surplus income to a long-term savings account that is invested in a fund, you need to be very mindful of anything that is left over. The only way of reversing Parkinson's law is to regularly review your income and expenditure and where there is surplus give it a job. If you don't your lifestyle will simply expand and it will disappear.

When we do this with clients they find that allocating this surplus income does not really impact their lifestyle. The money we are talking about here is being spent because it is there. It is not actually adding any significant value to your life, so when you strip it out and put it to good use elsewhere it doesn't dramatically change your lifestyle.

Now you've reached what I call your master plan. This is all the things you have in your control that create your financial future. There are no outside influences to this; it is all in your control.

What ifs

Once you have your plan you can start to think about things that might happen that are outside your control. For example, you might own a business and you hope to sell it one day but you don't know when. Or maybe you expect a gift or inheritance at some stage, but you don't know when or how much it will be. You might believe, but are not guaranteed, that you will get a promotion and pay rise.

What ifs are the area of a plan where you might let your mind run away with itself a little. They can be really useful because when we test our plan with them we see the impact they can have. You might think, 'If I just get the promotion I will be able to retire early', only to find it won't help you reach financial independence any sooner. Now you are going for the promotion because you want it and not because it makes any significant long-term financial difference.

Business owners love what ifs because, for many, it's the first time ever they have a way of working out how much is enough. This is often when I go head to head with their accountant. The scenario goes something like this: I have worked out that the client needs €800,000 from the sale of their business in order to reach financial independence. The accountant works out that the business is probably worth €1,000,000. An offer comes in for €900,000 and the accountant says it's 10% less than it is worth and I say it's €100,000 more than the client needs.

How do I do all the maths?

People always want to know how to figure out their date of financial independence. Remember, financial independence is the day in your life when you have created enough wealth that you don't have to work again and you don't have to worry about money. Figuring out how much is enough is a difficult task, with many complex inputs and many issues that need to be considered. It is a multi-factor calculation that I have spent the last 25+ years of professional life mastering. Luckily enough for you, AI has come along and it can do it all for you. I am not talking about expensive software; this is Microsoft Copilot, ChatGPT and sometimes plain old Google. We will go into this further in a minute, but basically any question you would ask me, any calculation you need done, you can ask the bot in language you understand and in seconds it will come back with an answer that will have a high degree of accuracy. You can ask it anything and it will give you an answer. It's not perfect, but it is an amazingly powerful tool and it is at your fingertips. Try it and you might be surprised.

Knowing what questions to ask is half the battle. Most people want to know when they will reach financial independence. But if you ask a bot just that you will get a random useless answer, so you need to be more precise and you need it to build in things for you. You need to accept that some things you do today will bring financial independence closer and others will push it further away. For example, if you do five safaris between now and financial independence you will probably reach financial independence later. On the other hand, if you move money sitting idle in a bank account into a well-constructed, well-diversified portfolio it is likely to move financial independence closer.

Another consideration is that if you are conservative with your estimates for growth then as each year passes and you achieve a return better on average than what your plan expected, financial independence will move closer. Accepting that markets will have a really tough time every three to five years, and accepting that one year in every four won't be positive, as long as the overall average is greater than your expected average growth rate you will get there quicker than expected.

I see this all the time in private practice when we start

working with a client. Let's say we establish that they will reach their date of financial independence by the time they are 62. They come back year after year for annual review and two things happen. First, they get older so they get closer to their financial independence age of 62. Second, on average their pensions and investments grow faster than we had built into the plan so financial independence also moves closer to them. Underestimating their salary increases, what bonuses they get and other factors also play a role in bringing financial independence closer.

Building a financial plan requires some guesswork. We know our guesses will sometimes be wrong, but we always try to guess on the right side of wrong. Some things are easy to guess, for example we guess 2% inflation. That's because the European Central Bank's role is to try to keep inflation at 2%. We all know that they don't achieve it every year, and we all feel it when they don't, but over long periods of time it's the best guess we have. But when it comes to things like what we expect pension and investment growth to be we really want to guess on the right side of wrong; in other words, we want to guess at a growth rate that turns out to be lower than the actual return.

If you are building your financial plan you will have to make some guesses, but make sure you guess on the right side of wrong. Be conservative with growth rates, expect the groceries to cost more than you think and expect that things will not go to plan. A financial plan is out of date the minute it's printed. That's the beauty of financial planning – it is dynamic.

We could all reach financial independence today if we upped sticks and went somewhere remote where we could live off grid, but most of us don't want to give up the comforts, the friendships and the lifestyle we are accustomed to. So one of the key things you need to figure out is how much money you will need to live your life when you stop working.

The best guide to this is to look at what you are spending today and really ask yourself if your lifestyle is going to change. When doing a financial plan for a client we have the luxury of expensive, powerful software that allows us to look at expenditure in a very dynamic way. Costs, for example college costs for kids, can be dropped into the financial plan for four years and then dropped out again. We know that people on average spend 35% less money at age 85 compared to what they were spending at 65, and although we don't cut expenditure at 85 by 35% (because we want to guess on the right side of wrong), we do target specific expenditures. So we drop the amount allocated to holidays and reduce or even eliminate the cost of running a car from age 85 onwards.

We have the luxury of this software, but for many years I did it in Excel and it was a grind. But the key to building any financial plan is that if you don't have absolute confidence in the individual inputs, if you don't question each of the component parts as you start to build the plan, it will be impossible for you to have confidence in your plan when it is completed.

Given that you won't have access to some of the tools a professional financial planner has, my suggestion is that you separate out specific goals, like funding college, and you allow for saving for them separately in your cash flow modelling. Do the same for mortgage repayments, etc. But when it comes to lifestyle costs and utilities, try to settle on one figure and don't make things too complicated; simply take that figure and use it.

This is where AI comes in. For this book I could have built a fancy calculator and guided you to my special 'book' website, captured your email address and stayed connected with you into the future. But that would be only serving myself. The reality is that AI is now part of our world. Even when you type a question into an ordinary Google search it throws out an AI-generated response as well as the 'traditional' responses. In other words, you don't even need an AI tool to use AI; Google already does it for you. But if you want to go a step further, downloading the free version of something like ChatGPT or Microsoft Copilot can be very useful.

If you're not familiar with AI, don't be daunted by it. The real beauty of AI is that you ask it questions like you would ask a friend or a professional.

The first thing I want you to work out is how much is enough?

I typed into an AI bot that it costs me €40,000 a year to live my life, I am 40 and I want to retire at 65. I asked it to allow for 2% inflation and tell me how much I will need at 65 to live comfortably. This is the exact response I got from one of the AI tools:

Calculating required lump sum at 65
To calculate the nominal amount needed at 65, start with the present value of €1,000,000 in today's euros. Adjusting for 2% inflation over 25 years: $(1.02)^{25}$ = 1.640, so the nominal amount required at 65 is €1,640,000.

I'll also ensure that assumptions about the 4% nominal return, 2% real return, and withdrawals starting at age 65 are clearly stated.

Summary of assumptions
Current annual living cost: €40,000.

Current age: 40; retirement age: 65; retirement length: 100 − 65 = 35 years.

Inflation: 2% per year.

Nominal investment return: 4% per year (implies a real return of 2% per year).

Withdrawals: annual, at end of each year, adjusted with inflation to preserve real purchasing power.

Required retirement pot expressed in today's euros (value at age 65 in real terms)
The required capital at age 65, expressed in today's (real) euros, is the present value at retirement of a 35year annuity paying €40,000 per year in real terms with a real return of 2%.

Annuity factor: $\text{AF}=\frac{1-(1+0.02)^{-35}}{0.02}\approx 25.0$

Required pot (real, at 65): $\text{Pot}_{\text{real}}=40{,}000\times 25.0 \;=\; \mathbf{€1{,}000{,}000}$

Required retirement pot as nominal euros at age 65 (actual euros you must have then)

Prices will have risen between now and age 65 by a factor $((1+0.02)^{25})$.

Growth factor to age 65: $(1.02)^{25}\approx 1.64$

Nominal pot required at age 65: $\text{Pot}_{65} = 1{,}000{,}000 \times 1.64 \;=\; \mathbf{€1{,}640{,}000}$

Quick interpretation

You need about €1,000,000 in today's euros at retirement to fund €40,000/year (real) for 35 years assuming a 2% real return.

That equals roughly €1.64 million in nominal euros at age 65 given 2% inflation over the next 25 years.

If you want alternatives

If you prefer a different investment return assumption or want withdrawals at the start of each year, I will recompute using that single changed assumption.

As you can see, it details its assumptions and walks you through the calculations. I think the response is robust, clear and gives us a great guide to where we are trying to get to. But you do need to be confident in the assumptions. Two things jumped out at me in the assumptions the AI bot used: the growth rate of 4% per annum; and the assumed safe withdrawal rate of 4% per annum.

If I were to go down the rabbit hole of safe withdrawal rates I could write an entire book on it (and many have been written, but only for financial nerds like me), but let me give you a simple explanation. The safe withdrawal rate for a fund is the percentage you can take from it each year and not run out of money by the end of the timeline. In English, that means how much you can safely take out of your pot and not be worried you are going to run out of money before you die.

I think the growth rate of 4% per annum is very fair but I wanted to test it at 4.5%. Despite the fact that our government has decided that 4% in your 60s and 5% from your 70s is the amount you have to take from pensions in Ireland, I think the 4% assumed by the bot as a safe withdrawal rate is just too high, so I want it to assume 3.2%, which is much more in line with European expectations. So I asked it to amend its response and the bot came back with this answer:

Organising the output

I'm considering how best to format everything. No need to use LaTeX unless it's for math expressions, but I should follow guidelines to keep things clear and compliant with developer rules.

I'll break the output into sections: Assumptions, Results (numbers), Interpretation, How much to save annually, and If you already have savings (optional). I'll stick to short paragraphs and ensure everything is concise, so it's easier to follow.

Assumptions

- Current annual living cost: €40,000.
- Current age: 40; retirement age: 65; retirement length: 35 years (65–100).
- Inflation: 2% per year.
- Nominal portfolio growth while saving: 4.5% per year.
- Safe withdrawal rate (first-year withdrawal as % of initial pot): 3.2%.
- No current retirement savings (if you have existing savings, see the note at the end).

First-year retirement spending at age 65 (nominal)
- Growth factor to age 65: $(1.02)^{25} \approx$ **1.6407**.

- First-year nominal spending at 65: €40,000 × 1.6407 = €65,628.

Required retirement pot at age 65 (nominal) using 3.2% SWR

Required pot = first-year spending / SWR = €65,628 / 0.032 = €2,050,875.

Required pot in nominal euros at age 65: €2,050,875.

Equivalent value in today's euros (real, at age 65 expressed in today's purchasing power)

Divide nominal pot by inflation growth factor: €2,050,875 / 1.6407 = €1,250,000.

Required pot in today's euros: €1,250,000.

How much you must save each year from age 40 to 65 (starting from zero) with 4.5% growth

- Future value target at 25 years: €2,050,875.
- Annual savings required (end-of-year deposits) using a 4.5% annual return:
    - PMT ≈ **€46,000 per year**.
    - Monthly equivalent = **€3,833 per month**.

> **Quick interpretation and practical notes**
>
> To maintain a €40,000 real lifestyle from 65 to 100 with 2% inflation and a 3.2% safe withdrawal rule you need about **€1.25M in today's euros**, which corresponds to **€2.05M nominal at 65**.
>
> If you already have retirement savings, the annual amount needed will be lower; if you plan to make changes to retirement age, expected returns, or withdrawal strategy, the required pot and yearly savings will change significantly.
>
> A 3.2% SWR is a conservative sustainability assumption; if you expect higher longterm real returns or accept more sequence-of-return risk, the required pot and savings could be different.

As you can see, the figure has risen from €1.6 million to over €2 million, which highlights the impact of getting your inputs right. It just shows how important it is that you are confident in your inputs.

As I was writing this I was going back over the figures and I realised that the bot had used two different phrases when it talked about growth. In one it said 'nominal return' and in the other it said 'return while saving'. This is very common when using AI – you have to double check everything! So I asked it why …

Summary of which growth assumptions were used

Yes. After you asked for 4.5% growth, I used a 4.5% nominal portfolio growth rate both during the accumulation phase (age 40–65) and during the withdrawal phase (age 65 onward) in the recalculations I gave.

Clarification about real vs nominal returns

A 4.5% nominal return with 2% inflation corresponds to a real return of approximately 2.45098% (calculated as (1.045/1.02) − 1). I used that real rate when converting nominal cashflows into inflation-adjusted (real) terms for the annuity-style calculation.

Notes about the two methods and consistency

- In the 'savings to a target' / PMT calculation I used 4.5% nominal for the portfolio growth while saving to age 65.
- In the SWR calculation I used the same 4.5% nominal return from age 65 onward when interpreting how the portfolio would grow while withdrawals were taken.
- In the annuity-style calculation I converted the 4.5% nominal to the 2.45098% real return and used that real rate for the 35year inflation-indexed withdrawal stream.

If you want a single table of inputs and the exact formulas I used I will produce that now if you want it.

I imagine that having looked at the responses you are now scared. You need over €1,250,000 in today's money to have €40,000 a year. Although it is not a perfect answer, it really isn't at all bad. It has ignored the state pension, which isn't a bad thing, it has assumed (because I told it to) that spending will start at €40,000 a year and increase each year in line with inflation. However, we know from the statistics that spending increases for the first two years after retirement before dropping gradually year by year until it reaches 35% less at 85 compared to 65. But the beauty of the bot is you can go back repeatedly asking it to refine its assumptions and it will never refuse to answer.

My suggestion for you at this stage is to draft a detailed question outside the bot, for example in Word, and then paste it into at least two bots and see what response you get. Here's one I prepared earlier:

> I want you to act as my financial planner, use Irish law and Irish tax when compiling your plan.
>
> **Personal details**
> I am a 40-year-old single male.
>
> **Income**
> I earn €50,000 per annum after tax.
>
> **Expenditure**
> My cost of living is €30,000 per annum, excluding my mortgage.

Savings
I have €8,000 in a bank account.

Debt
I have €220,000 left on my mortgage and it costs me €1,179 per month. The rate is 4.15%. I have no other debt.

Assets
My home is worth €450,000 and I have a car worth €12,000.

Pension
I have a pension with €80,000 in it. I pay €350 per month into it and my employer matches it.

My goals
I want to retire at 65 and maintain my current standard of living, which costs €30,000 per annum.

I want to go on a big holiday in five years and in ten years for my 45th and 50th birthdays. These will cost €5,000 each.

I want to change the car every six years and I will need €10,000 cash to do that.

Assumptions
Assume 2% inflation on my expenses. Assume my wages will increase at a rate of 2.5% per annum and assume pensions and investments will grow at 4.5% per annum. I also want you to assume that I will increase

my contribution to savings investment by 2% per annum and that I want to prioritise maximising my pension contributions within the age-restricted limits as set out by Revenue. Assume I will die aged 100.

Requirement
Build me a plan that will see me meet my cost of living requirements, pay my mortgage, achieve my goals and retire at 65. If it is not all possible please push back my retirement age to an appropriate age.

I typed this once and added it to a free AI tool. I wanted my experience to be as close to yours as possible. This is the response I got:

Thanks for providing such detailed information, Eoin. Based on your current financial situation, goals, and assumptions – and using Irish tax and pension rules – here's a summary of your **financial plan** and key insights:
Summary of Your Financial Profile
- **Age:** 40
- **Net Income:** €50,000/year (growing at 2.5% annually)
- **Living Expenses:** €30,000/year (excluding mortgage, inflating at 2%)

- **Mortgage:** €220,000 remaining, €1,179/month, 4.15% interest, 25 years left
- **Savings:** €8,000 in bank
- **Pension:** €80,000 current value, €350/month + €350 employer match
- **Assets:** Home (€450,000), Car (€12,000)
- **Goals:**
  - Retire at 65 and maintain current lifestyle (inflation-adjusted)
  - €5,000 holidays at age 45 and 50
  - Replace car every 6 years for €10,000
  - Maximise pension contributions within Revenue limits

Key Findings from the Financial Projection
- You are **on track to meet your goals until retirement**, including mortgage payments, holidays, and car replacements.
- You are **maximising pension contributions** within Revenue limits (25% of income for your age group).
- Your **retirement fund (pension + savings)** grows steadily until age 65.
- However, **your retirement fund will be depleted before age 100,** meaning **your current plan does not fully support retirement at 65.**

Recommendations

To ensure you can retire comfortably and maintain your lifestyle until age 100, consider one or more of the following:

1. Delay Retirement

- **New suggested retirement age: 67–68**
- This allows more time to grow your pension and savings, and reduces the number of years you'll need to fund retirement.

2. Increase Pension Contributions

- You're currently contributing €8,400/year (employee + employer).
- At age 50, your allowable contribution increases to **30% of income**, and later to **35–40%**.
- Consider making **Additional Voluntary Contributions (AVCs)** to reach the maximum allowable limit.

3. Boost Savings

- Increase your annual savings rate beyond the current 2% growth.
- Consider investing in tax-efficient vehicles like **PRSA** or **RACs** for additional relief.

4. Downsize or Monetise Assets

- Your home is worth €450,000. If needed, downsizing or equity release could provide additional retirement income.

Next Steps

Would you like:

- A **detailed year-by-year breakdown** of your financial plan?
- A **graphical report** showing your savings, pension, and retirement fund over time?
- Help setting up **AVCs** or choosing investment options?

Let me know how you'd like to proceed, and I'll tailor the next part of your plan accordingly.

I think this is quite a good response. The only major mistake the bot made was the suggestion regarding maximising pension contributions and also paying into a PRSA/RAC – you can't do both. Your age-related maximums are the most you can put in. But other than that it was a quite good first attempt.

Now I requested a year-by-year breakdown and identified a few errors. First, the salary didn't stop when I retired. Neither did the contribution to the pension, so we fixed that. The bot had also assumed that I needed to change the car this year, so I told it to wait six years before doing that. The reason I did that was because the bot had allowed me to go into negative cash flow and didn't highlight I would need to borrow for this.

Once these things were fixed the bot highlighted that if I retired at 65 I would run out of money at age 80. This is the chart that went with it:

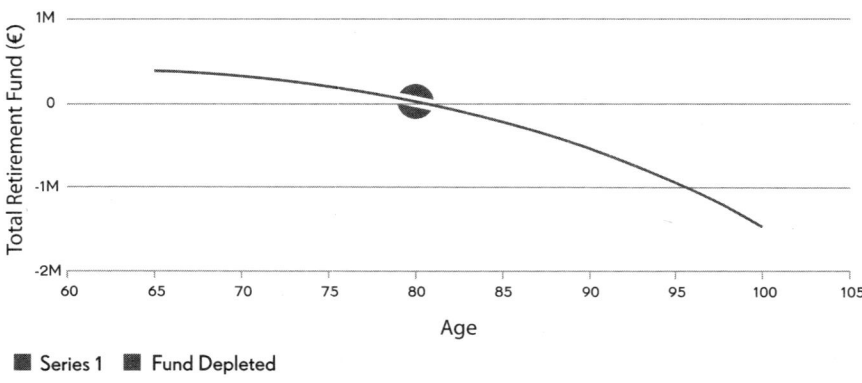

So I asked it what age could I retire at; in other words I wanted it to work out my date of financial independence. It came back to me with an age of 73 and said I would not run out of money before 100 if all the other assumptions proved to be true.

Finally, I reminded it that we are assuming growth on pensions and investment of 4.5% and I asked what growth would be required in order to be able to retire at 65 and not run out of money before 100 years of age. It told me 8.72% and, in fairness, it flagged that this is aggressive and would require higher-risk investments to give it any chance of success.

I am not trying to give you a 'how to' AI guide here. I am

simply trying to show you the powerful tools that are available at your fingertips and I am using a free version that's accessible to all. There are other tools out there that you can use and pay for.

I would say this would have been really useful for me when I was building all my financial plans in Excel. AI is very powerful and it is great for building basic financial plans or doing the maths on things you can express in words but don't know how to build a function in Excel or punch into a calculator.

Overall I think AI is a powerful tool that will only get better with time, but I do have a few words of warning:

1. It does not always get it right. If something doesn't seem right, remember it won't take offence if you ask it, 'Are you right on …?'
2. It will only answer what you ask it. If your questions are not clear you won't get a clear answer. For example, I would need to go back into the calculation given here and ask it to do it all over again because tax has been ignored on the growth.
3. Speak to it like a friend or professional – it makes it easier on you and the bot.
4. Get your assumptions right.
5. Use more than one AI tool so you can ask it the same thing and compare results. I happen to use ChatGPT and Microsoft Copilot, but I do not claim for one second to be an expert in AI. I have no idea if they are the best, the worst or average. But I have found they sometimes give me different answers, and when

they do I tell them that: 'Copilot/ChatGPT gave me a different answer'; and I tell the bot what the answer was. It will explain which of them is wrong and why. I have had it say the other was right and they are wrong and it corrects its answer.

6. It is incredibly useful but it is not a human: use it, but tread very carefully and double check everything.
7. The biggest problem with using a bot is that we don't know what we don't know. A human might say 'Have you thought about X?', but a bot is less likely to raise this. However, if you asked it 'Is there anything else I should consider?' it will often offer some decent suggestions as to what you are missing.
8. Right now the bots get their information from lots of places on the internet, but they are more heavily reliant on certain sources of information. My limited knowledge tells me that things like Reddit posts are, surprisingly, right up there as a source, as are press releases, Google reviews and government websites and publications. Interestingly, the bots are also believed to suffer recency bias, placing more importance on recent information than on older information on the same topic.
9. I think the more factual your query the more useful the bot's answer is. Asking for opinions is less helpful. In my opinion.
10. Do not make life decisions based on the answers you get.

Revisiting your plan

Building your financial plan is great, but once you hit save on the final version it is out of date. Financial planning is a dynamic process and you can't just build your financial plan, put it to one side and never revisit it. Legislation changes, your goals change, your income and your expenditure change. So too does your financial plan and you need to keep on top of it.

In general I think we should all spend 15–20 minutes a week working on our finances. When it comes to your financial plan you should do a mini review after six months and a full review and possibly a rebuild after a year and then repeat.

A mini review is simply a quick look to see if you are on track and if anything major has changed. A full annual review is more in-depth; you question everything again and possibly do a rebuild.

Keeping up to date

Legislation, product changes, new entrants, even trends change all the time and it is important to stay on top of them. A perfect example of this in Ireland is PRSAs (a type of pension), which have changed twice in the last three years. The government changed the rules around PRSAs, which meant a flood of people taking advantage of the rule change. Then government bowed to pressure from the opposition and changed the rules again. They didn't go back to what they were, but made another change that closed off the big advantage they had created two years earlier.

The technicalities of this don't actually matter. The fact is that there was a two-year window that was very advantageous to some, but not advantageous for enough people that it would make the mainstream media. So that means you or your financial planner would need to have been aware of it.

This happens from time to time and the window can be short. If you are going to take control of your finances without using a financial planner all the burden is on you. But even if you have a financial planner who is on top of this stuff it is still good for you to keep yourself informed. Keep an eye on social media accounts like mine, or weekly columns like mine! But go beyond me an seek out your own panel of people you trust in the old school and new school media. Just make sure the information you are being given is being provided by somebody qualified to give it.

Consider using an adviser

If you're thinking of going it alone, honestly my admiration goes out to you. I am a professional financial planner and there is no other profession I would be willing to step into part time in order to save a few quid and look after it myself. When I need a professional I use one. Whether that's painting the house, fixing the car, getting my will done or fixing my teeth I am happy that somebody who does this all day, every day will have the skill and expertise to do the job professionally. I know it will be done properly, quickly and professionally and I am happy to pay someone to do what they're good at. More important, I recognise that there is stuff I don't know I don't know, and somebody who does a particular job all the time will be able to see around corners, corners that I don't even know exist.

But when it comes to financial planning I also believe it is about being accountable to somebody else. If you are going it alone and you know there is somebody in your life, whether a partner, family member or friend, who you can sit down and discuss it with, that might be a solution. But only if you respect them and you will feel accountable to that person. The same goes for the financial planner you pick if you decide to go down that route.

The tools at your fingertips are excellent and getting better all the time, but getting that bot to build a financial plan showed me that right now they are only useful up to a point. However, in other cases AI can give completely wrong advice, advice that is not implementable. But I remember how hard it was to build a financial plan in Excel, and how tedious it was to make amendments to a plan when somebody changed job or came into money or something else changed; you literally had to start again from scratch.

I am trying to be as balanced as I possibly can. If you really want to do it yourself I am trying to give you the best helping hand I can. I genuinely hope you achieve all you want to achieve.

But ultimately I went into this profession because I want to help people get the most out of their money. I want to build financial plans that have my clients' money supporting the life they want to have and I want the privilege of getting to check in on the progress of that year by year as the plan develops. I get to help people through the worst times of their life and the best times and I never underestimate the privilege I have being a financial planner. I believe the work of a good financial planner is worth its weight in gold and I think everyone should have one. But of course you might say 'Sure he would say that.'

Back in the 'Big mistakes' section I mentioned the fact that people who have a financial planner have 2.5 times the net worth of people who don't when they retire and I asked you to think about why that might be. There could be several reasons: maybe the people who engage with a financial planner have a bit of net worth to start with (likely); or maybe the financial planner made all the right calls with investments and pensions and other decisions and so the client got richer (less likely).

Or maybe it comes down to accountability. There was a piece of research done in relation to pets and prescriptions. If we as humans are given a prescription for medicine for something that is wrong with us we are less likely to follow that prescription than we are to adhere to a prescription that our vet gave us for our pets. In other words, we are more likely to look after our pets than ourselves. This might be because we feel more accountable to our pet; we feel an obligation to them that we don't feel as strongly as we do for ourselves. I believe the same is true of the relationship with a good financial planner. When you engage with a good one and you stick with them over a long period, you get satisfaction from sticking with the plan. You don't just create it and put it away; you meet with a planner on a regular basis, which means you are constantly adjusting your plan and taking advantage of different situations as they arise. The reality is there are things you don't know you don't know. Legislation changes, products change, sometimes even trends make a difference to how you should be behaving, and a good financial planner's job is to stay on top of all this and adjust your plan to make sure you make the most of the money you have.

Financial stress

Whether you go it alone or engage a planner, money can be stressful. I have seen people smothered under the pressure they feel about money. I have seen people lose weight, split up with their partners, and I have had people in my life who I have been very, very worried about.

Money is often a symptom but sometimes it is not the cause of the stress. The root cause is often something else that resulted in money problems; then the money problems either create cracks in other parts of your life or the money problems simply expose the cracks that were being brushed over.

The problem is whether money is the cause or the symptom doesn't actually matter, because when you have money problems there is no getting away from them. They are everywhere. They control what you do, what you eat, who you see, how you live. Everything in our lives is interconnected with money.

There is an entire book (maybe my next one) on dealing with financial stress, but I do want to give you a few pointers on the first steps to take to prevent money issues creeping in.

Or if you find yourself struggling, maybe these few short words will send you off on a journey of discovery that will lift you out of how you are feeling.

1. Have a buffer

We have talked about your buffer repeatedly in this book. That's because it is important. It is your financial security blanket. It is what helps you sleep at night and it is the foundation stone of your entire financial structure.

Get it right and you are invincible financially. Get it wrong and those financial punches are just going to keep coming, wave after wave.

The buffer doesn't care how much you earn or how much savings you have; it is there for everyone. I have yet to come across anyone who put the effort into using the strategy properly who didn't feel it was worth the effort. Most people say it's a game-changer.

2. Talk to yourself

When you are having difficulties, don't ignore them. Write them down and look at the actual situation. When you write it down it might be better than you think, which will be great. It also might be worse – but you didn't make it worse by writing it down. Things were always that way, but at least now you know what you are dealing with.

If you can map a way out, great, but I don't believe there is any financial situation, good or bad, that is made better by keeping it to yourself.

3. Talk to someone else

Over the last 15 years society has done an amazing job at getting rid of the stigma around mental health. Now we know it is okay to not be okay. No matter who you are. Even big butch blokes are okay about telling others how they are feeling. This is a great thing and I am delighted we have got here.

But there is still a stigma around talking about money. We love to hear about other people's money but we rarely open up about our own. If you are okay financially and have no worries, statistically there is a higher probability that one of your friends, family or peers is not in a great place and could do with someone to talk to.

Will you accept a challenge? In the next week, talk to someone about money, someone you have never spoken to about money before. I am not asking you to share your payslip or bank statements; just bring up the topic with somebody. Blame me if you like – tell them you read this book and I challenged you. Say something like 'What's the best financial decision you ever made?' or 'What's your relationship with money like?'

By doing this you are pushing on a door and you will find out whether or not that person is open to this conversation. But maybe more important, they will now know that you are open to talking about money. If either of you ever needs each other again you both know that door is open.

By doing this one conversation at a time I believe we can get a society that doesn't talk about money talking about money.

4. Set goals

Sometimes our money can stress us out simply because we feel a little lost and we have no direction. Setting goals is the first step in addressing this problem. At least now you know where you are trying to get to.

Sometimes we set big goals and we feel good about them, but then the drudgery of trying to achieve those goals kicks in and we feel deflated again. If you are setting a big goal that is more than a year away you must give yourself little rewards along the way.

Let's say you're saving for a house. You might come with a rule that says, 'If I save consistently for three months I get to splurge on X', whatever your X might be. These little rewards keep us engaged and motivated to keep going. Only you can decide what your X is and only you can decide how often you need to be rewarded; unfortunately I can't help you with that.

5. Control your money

I won't apologise for repeating this. You either control your money or it controls you. Decide. If you haven't got control now, do something before you go to bed tonight that takes even a tiny bit of control back. It doesn't matter what it is or how small it is. Switch a utility bill and save money. Review your spending over the last week. Work out every job for every euro in your bank account between now and your next pay day. Or set up a standing order to put a fiver into savings every month from now on. I don't care how small it is, if you feel you're controlled by money, flip the switch and take the control back.

Conclusion

We started this book with me getting brain surgery at a time in my life when I was very unhappy. As I write these final pages, I am reflecting on all that has happened in the last seven years. There are certainly some things that I really wish had been different, but so much good has happened.

I brought Colin Duignan in as CEO of Prosperous and he has taken us from four staff to forty staff in the last four years and we will add at least another ten in the next twelve months. We have seen serious growth over the first three years with Colin at the helm and as I write, approaching the end of year four, we are on track to have 100% growth this year.

I am back doing what I love to do: working with my clients; helping Colin at board level; doing my work on radio, TV and corporate speaking; writing books; and doing my Q&A every Saturday on Instagram.

My fitness has taken a hit as I tried to get this book done but

I am determined to get back on track in the next few months. But I have had some amazing success with my health since my accident. I have run two marathons and as I write I am wondering which one I will go for next. I am really looking forward to having time to concentrate on my health and fitness again now that this book is complete!

It has not been all sunshine and lollipops; there are some really big things in my life that I wish were in a better place. But that's life.

Of everything that has happened since I banged my head, what I am most happy about is Clara. As I write this last paragraph, it is a Saturday evening. She is pottering around upstairs getting ready for a work trip to London tomorrow. I'm downstairs typing away. We bought a home together a few months ago and we love where we live. We are happy.

... Oh, and we're getting married.

Acknowledgements

It's hard to narrow down who and what should be acknowledged for the information in this book because it's a career of engagements with my colleagues, product providers, peers and competitors combined with all the amazing client interactions I have had in over 25 years working in this profession that bring the information and knowledge all together. I learn from others and simply pass it on to you.

There is however a team of people who worked specifically on this book, Deirdre and Lisa at Eriu, and the team at Gill Hess definitely deserve a mention as do Megan and both Niamhs in NK Management, thank you all.

Colin and the team in Prosperous also allowed me the headspace to go and work on it, but more importantly they listened to me moan about how the book is doing my head in!

I should acknowledge my mother. Whilst writing this book I fully recognised for the first time that, although I got my business acumen from Dad, any compassion or empathy I might have has come from my mother. Thanks Mam.

Lastly and of most importance, Clara. More than anyone you listened to me moan and you were my sounding board for some of the stories I was putting in. You were the litmus test for my explanations. You even managed to get excited about the stats and other stuff that I was excited about. Your input, feedback, guidance and tolerance didn't go unnoticed. Your acceptance of the disruption to our lives that this book caused was very much appreciated. Clara, thank you for being you, I wouldn't be here without you and I can't wait for what comes next for us.